Maliek

Part One

Katreka Carter

𝒦𝒶𝓁𝒶𝓃𝒾 ℬ𝑜𝑜𝓀𝓈

Maliek

Part One

No part of this book may be reproduced in any form without permission in writing from the publisher.

Printed in the United States of America

© Copyright 2012 by Katreka Carter
All Rights reserved.
ISBN 978-0692636176

PROLOGUE

Don't ever think in life that you can't find true love. As you read this book, you will find out that there is someone out there for everyone. Real love is predestined. When fate finds you, your heart will know it right away. Maliek Montana was a drug lord and a prominent business owner of Club Stallion. He dated the top actresses and models across the country. He was wealthy yet he was still a lonely young man. One day he was sitting in his office working and he glanced up at his television monitor.

Who in the world is that? He said to himself.

She was so beautiful and innocent looking. He called down to his bartender so that he could find out who this goddess was. Once he met Ms. Jada James, his life took a new turn. When one of his former employees (Charlie Jackson aka CJ) kidnapped her, he knew at that point he was truly in love with her. Maliek would soon find out that CJ had more than one vendetta against him.

Relax and enjoy the story of true love, romance and betrayal.

By Katreka Carter

CHAPTER 1

If anyone would have told me that I'd wind up with Maliek Montana, I would have thought they were lying. I came from a very strict religious background and my dad died when I was twelve years old, which made my family extremely close.

My mom, Mrs. Clara James, continued to raise my brother Aaron and me in a middle class neighborhood. We did not have everything, but we did not want for anything either. My mom didn't play. I can remember her saying that if we didn't go to church, we shouldn't expect to do any extra activities. I also remember my half-grown behind saying under my breath that I'd be glad when I became an adult.

My brother, Aaron, was five years my senior. He teased me a lot. Aaron went to college and shortly after that, got drafted into the NFL. In the very early part of his career, he got injured. I remember it like it was just yesterday: mom and I were jumping up and down, cheering him on like cheerleaders, when he got tackled by three humongous guys that looked like they were raised on corn. He laid there and didn't move.

My mom screamed, "what have they done to my baby?" We cried and screamed trying to get out of our seats. The next thing I knew, he was being carried out on a gurney. It was a horrible day. When we got to the hospital, Aaron was already in surgery. The doctor came over to us and said "Ms. James, there is no internal damage but he has permanent damage to both of his knees."

The NFL paid him off very well, but that was the end of his pro football career. Even though he'd gotten hurt, he still achieved his goal. I felt sorry for my brother, but that only meant one thing: he was home with me and mom again, and he and I sometimes didn't get along very well. Because of this, I looked forward to going off to college somewhere.

CHAPTER 2

After my senior year of high school, I was accepted into Michigan State University. I majored in Business Administration. I could not believe that my best friend Chianti had enrolled in the same college. We had been best friends in junior high school until her family moved to Atlanta, GA. It was so wonderful that we ended up together again. We often said we wanted to attend the same college, and now had the chance to be roommates.

After I graduated with my Bachelor's degree, I moved to Detroit. I landed a management job with Chase Bank. With all my savings, I purchased a nice condo. I knew that I was all grown up now and there wasn't anything anyone could tell me. I was young, beautiful and shapely. I was 5ft 5 inches tall, had caramel-colored skin. My hair was naturally silky, long, black and hung down to my shoulders. My eyes were light brown and I had very long eye lashes that almost looked fake. I was glamorous and loved to smell good at all times. A year later, I got a call from my best friend Chichi saying she was on her way to Detroit.

It was cool that she was coming, especially since she had also gotten a job with a large law firm. We were roommates again. Chi Chi was a too hot to trot sister. She was 5ft 7inches tall, with one of the sharpest original short hair cut hair styles since Halle Berry. Her body was shaped like a coca cola bottle. As she swayed in her walk, her hips stood out. I had always teased her and she would say, "You are not short stopping."

We always kept up with the latest clubs and the hottest entertainment in Detroit, Chicago and Wisconsin.

CHAPTER 3

One day Chi Chi and I were reclining on my burgundy leather sofa during our free time. She would take one end and I would take the other. I was reading one of the news magazines I had just subscribed to. It had a list of the hottest new bachelors and what they did for a living.

"Girl, check this out, Club Stallion. Look at this young man!"

Chi Chi got up and came to see. After taking a glance she said, "Wow, that's thick."

My eyes just got glued to the picture in front of me. This brother had it really going on. He was so fine that he had the most succulent lips I had ever seen.

"Chi Chi, I think we had better check this club out."

She saw the sincere expression on my face.

"Girl, don't tell me you want to go meet the man of your dreams."

"Yes that's exactly what I'm going to do." I pointed at his picture.

Chi Chi told me that he had been featured in the Ebony and Essence magazines. I don't know how I hadn't read about him before, considering how much I read those magazines.

"Chi Chi, is it Stiletto Night or what?"

We gave each other high fives and went into our separate rooms to get dressed. I decided to wear an Enyce jean cut fit with the swimsuit crisscross blouse and matching jean and beige short cut boots. My hair was freshly done making it bouncy as I walked. Chi Chi wore a Baby Phat jean skirt with the matching jacket and tall stiletto boots.

"We'll take my car, besides I love to drive."

My car was the best gift I had ever received for my graduation from my mom and brother. It was a brand new Benz, 500 SEL convertible. That was the happiest day of my life. I recall walking from the venue where the graduation had been held, to the parking lot, only to find it sitting there with a banner that read "congratulations Jada." I left the banner on till it faded.

We got into the car and headed to the club. Once we arrived, we saw all kinds of stretched limos, Benzes, Jags, and Cadillac's parked outside. The club also had valet parking available. Chi Chi said, "Girl are you sure they don't have a concert going on or something?"

We were extremely excited. The smell of arrogance and money was in the air. There was a large billboard with elegant lights that said "Welcome to Club Stallion, where we welcome all Stallions." I immediately said to her

"They must be talking about me. The owner must know me or something."

Little did I know that down the road, I would become his number one girl. We drove up in front of the club and a couple of gentlemen approached the car, dressed in Armani suits and shoes that cost at least $2500. They opened our doors and one said, "Welcome to Club Stallion. My name is Goldie." He handed me a ticket and proceeded to valet my car. *Wow, this is what I'm talking about.*

When we got to the door the cover charge was $100 per person. That was not a problem for us since we hadn't been out in a long time and we owed it to ourselves. We had been all work and no play.

There were two men collecting money at the door dressed in the same attire as the gentlemen outside. This club was the class of all classes. We stood in amazement. We stepped through the doors. The club was exquisite and everyone was well fit. It had three floors. The top floor was for the laid back executive types or true ballers. Every man that calls himself a baller doesn't have to sell drugs. Some people just make honest money and love to spend it. Most of the guys on the third floor love to gamble and don't want to mix with the other crowds on the other floors. To be on this floor, you had to be a member, which you could become by purchasing annual membership.

A lot of the NFL and NBA players took full advantage of this floor. They had their own private key car which gave them full access to everything. This also included access to private rooms for whatever suited their moods.

The second floor was VIP. It featured several rooms with massage parlors and hot tubs. Like the third floor, it also had a directory which provided companionship services. The companions were from all different nationalities, shapes and sizes. Nobody had to party alone.

The first floor was slamming with three bars. There was a waterfall at the center of the club that flowed from the top to the bottom of the floor. This place was out of sight and from what I saw, there were some real gentlemen here, and that was what we really liked. People spoke to us as we walked passed them and they were generous. The women were equally pleasant, which was different from a lot of clubs we had been to. There were no hoochies waiting in lines to use the restroom. All I wanted was to see the owner.

CHAPTER 4

Everywhere we looked, there were well-dressed men and women. We spotted two seats at the bar so we took them. As soon as we were seated, Chi Chi nudged me on my side and nodded her head at the fine looking bartender. He was dressed in black and white. His hair was short and curly. He was also bowlegged, which was right up Chi Chi's alley. The bartender approached us and said, "How are you ladies doing this evening?" As he looked directly at Chi Chi. You could see the sudden spark between them.

"What can I get you ladies?" Nobody responded, so I decided to break the ice by saying, "I'll have a glass of Remy Martin with lemon juice."

Chi Chi ordered a shot of Hennessy on the rocks. The bartender later returned with our drinks decorated with umbrellas.

"My name is CJ."

He extended his hand toward Chi Chi and as he took her hand, he kissed it. She turned to me and smiled. She then responded, "My name is Chianti, but everyone calls me Chi Chi, and this is my best friend Jada."

"It's a pleasure to meet both of you. You both look really nice. What are you ladies up to this evening?"

"Thank you, we are just out being grown."

We all laughed. CJ's eyes were always on Chi Chi and her eyes on him. He would go to assist other customers but he would be right back to us.

CHAPTER 5

Maliek was sitting upstairs in this office counting money and doing his paper work. He happened to glance at his television monitor that showed everyone in the club from all angles. He could zoom in or zoom out on their faces. He switched the monitor to where CJ was working and zoomed in on a face. He was mesmerized by a certain woman's beauty.

Huh, look a here, look a here, where did she come from? He watched her as she bounced in her seat to the beat of the music playing. *I want to know who she is. You talking about a ten.* The telephone behind the bar began to ring and CJ answered it.

"Run it," he said. He turned his attention towards us while he was talking. We couldn't her exactly what he was saying but he continued to nod his head and smile at the same time. He hung up and walked back to where we were sitting.

"Did you say your name was Jada?"

"Yes is there something wrong?"

"No there is nothing wrong. My boss just called to find out who you were."

I got so nervous and I could feel a tingle in my stomach.

"He said everything is on the house and if you all get a little hungry, our restaurant is around this corner. He wants you to order whatever you want off the menu when you are ready."

CJ turned to wait on another customer.

"Girl did you hear what he said?"

"Yeah girl," Chi Chi said.

We were both very excited.

"I guess the man is watching you. He must have this place monitored. You just can't see him."

I put on my sexy look and said to her, "You know it. Now I really got to give it to him."

I started my own little beat with hands on my hips. Several guys walked up to ask the two of us to dance. We both love to step and we had always felt as if no one could out step us.

Finally the DJ started playing the chocolate factory and I definitely couldn't stand it any longer. Chi Chi looked at me and said, "Take the floor girl." I knew I had to put my all into it because I was being watched by Mr. Man himself. I was going to make this memorable. I gave Chi Chi the right thumbs up and told her to watch this new move as I began to double spin. The young man told me his name was Lester but I didn't care what his name was because I wanted to meet one man and one man only. Besides, I had already caught his eye from a distance. There is nothing wrong with a substitute when you are trying to get what you want. Lester could really step and he had it going on.

I strutted back to the bar trying to keep my composure, when I saw Chi Chi and CJ in deep conversation. I sat down and drank my drink. I watched CJ put his rap down on her, leaning over her and I acted like I didn't even notice them. Where was Mr. Man himself? Why hadn't he come down to meet me personally? I was thinking about him and watching CJ rubbing the inside of Chi Chi's hand. She looked over at me and I just shook my head. It didn't matter to me because I was really enjoying the setting. I was really happy for her since she had been through so many relationships.

I remember her second year in college when she was dating the captain of the football team, Jay Sanford. He was a very popular guy and everyone wanted a piece of him. He had claimed to be crazy about her. One evening, Chi Chi went to his football practice to surprise him. She walked onto the field and didn't see him. She asked his teammates if they had seen Jay, and one of his teammates who didn't get much attention pointed her towards the direction of the gym. She walked to the gym and didn't see a soul in sight. All of a sudden as she turned to walk out, she heard a lot of moaning: "Oh, oh Jay."

She recognized Dana's voice, an MSU cheerleader. She walked to the side of the bleachers and that's when her world was blown apart. She saw that love of her life bending someone else over. Jay quickly moved and stopped doing what he was doing, but it was too late. Looking embarrassed he said, "Chi Chi, I'm sorry, let me explain how this slut tried to seduce me."

"Stop lying you are busted!" Tears streamed down her face. "I came here to surprise you with two tickets to one of your favorite recording artist's, Jaheim's concert, and this is what I get in return?"

She tore up the tickets and slapped him across his face with them. "You are nasty!"

Dana tore off running like she was in the Olympics. And Chi Chi hollered, "You don't have to run, you can have this trick!"

Her whole world had been crushed. Just to see her take interest in someone made me happy for her. If it worked out, fine if not, that was okay too. At this very moment she looked happy and was full of smiles.

CHAPTER 6

As the evening progressed, CJ had Chi Chi magnetized. At this point, they looked very content with each other, but I wasn't, because I wanted to meet Maliek. After being lost in my own thoughts, I cleared my throat and CJ said, "What's wrong?" "I didn't mean to interrupt you two, but I think I am ready to order some food." I knew the alcohol would take over my body and I would get tipsy. He reached under the bar and pulled out a menu.

Chi Chi was busy, so I ordered her the same thing I ordered for myself. We usually liked to eat the same types of food, especially when it comes to fast food. When the food came, it was decorated like it cost a thousand dollars. There were jumbo shrimp with all kinds of sauces, freshly cut potatoes and a salad with ranch and bleu cheese dressing. There was also an ice bucket with a bottle of Crystal, along with a vase that had six red roses and a card that read, "I would like to meet you but I can't come down at this time," *compliments of Maliek Montana*. I thought it was cute.

CJ then said, "My boss wants you to leave your phone number with me so he can call you if it's ok with you." I reached in my purse and gave him my business card and said, "Give this to Mr. Mystery man and tell him to make it soon."

"I sure will because if I don't, he will have my head," He replied.

I knew for sure that there was a connection with CJ and Chi Chi when I saw her give him her card. If only Maliek would just come down and walk past me, I would be happy. But I guess good things come to those who wait.

When Chi Chi and I got home, we talked until we were out of words. I was the first to say goodnight. In the morning, I got dressed and left for a little church I had found, but I hadn't decided to become a member yet. The name of the church was Community Church of God In Christ. The pastor was Elder Trells. The church was not a very big one, but the pastor was an anointed preacher and the people were very friendly. There were plenty of young people under 30, and I really liked that. I felt like I belonged.

His sermon was on "Waiting on God." He said that when we wait on God, everything always turns out for the good. The message was good but I had other things on my mind. I kept asking myself how I could wait on God when I longed to have someone in my life. Maybe I had waited long enough and this was my time. I was tired of being alone. I truly believed the pastor. He also said that if we didn't wait, we would usually end up in a bad situation.

On my way home I stopped by my favorite soul food restaurant called *Steve's*. They already knew me by name. Their food was so good that it would make you slap someone. I stood at the counter clicking my heels like a child waiting for some candy.

"Ms. James, what can I get for you today?" said the smiling waitress.

"You can get me the Sunday Special," I said. The Sunday Special was barbeque chicken, dressing, mac n cheese, and peach cobbler dessert.

Steve walked up to me.

"Where have you been?"

"I have been around. My best friend moved here and she usually cooks a lot of soul food meals at home. She's a southern girl."

"Oh I see," He said.

"This is one of those Sundays that we are lazy, but as you can see, I haven't forgot about you all."

"That's nice to hear. Come and see us again. He said as I passed him a fifty dollar bill. He gave me my change and I headed home.

While I drove home, I thought about how I needed to work out three times a week because I didn't want to lose my shape. I had to keep myself tight, and so far, I had been doing very well, especially since Chi Chi cooked all the time. When I got home, we had dinner and it was delicious.

"Girl, how did you know I wasn't going to cook today?"

"Because I know when you sleep through breakfast, what time it is; now how long have I known you?"

"You think you know me Jada?" she said smiling. She knew I was telling the truth.

"I know you, just like I knew you like CJ from the other night and all the attention he was giving you."

"Well you still don't know yet. You can't judge a book by its cover. He could be something else other than the other night."

After we were done eating and cleaning up, I slipped into something comfortable and we decided to watch the movie *Dreamgirls* again. The previous night, the movie seemed to be watching us, but this time we managed to stay awake. Jennifer Hudson and Beyonce were the bomb, especially when Jennifer sang "You're The Best Man I've Ever Known." We stood up on the sofa singing along as if we were on Broadway. It was hilarious. Eventually it came time to turn in for the night. Tomorrow was another work day. Monday's and Friday's were the busy days at my job.

CHAPTER 7

After we finished our last drinks for the evening, Chi Chi asked me if it was ok for me to drive. I wondered why she would ask me such a question, because she knew for as long as we had been friends, I had always been the designated driver. We said our goodbyes to CJ and he held Chi Chi's hand as if he didn't want to let it go. Finally, we walked out of the club as if we owned it.

As I looked in my purse for the valet ticket, my car appeared out of nowhere. Maliek was definitely watching me and he must have called the valet to have my car ready by the time I was outside. This man was too much. This is what I called a club with all the trimmings.

"Did you ladies have a nice time?" Goldie asked. Chi Chi didn't have to say anything. But I did.

"Yes, we most certainly did and we will be back real soon." As we got into my car, I rolled down the window and said to him, "thank you again, and have a good night."

"Girl I can't believe that club. Can you?" I asked

"No girl, and all of those fine men in one place is unbelievable. And I haven't experienced that much fun and generosity in God knows when."

I stared straight ahead in my own world while driving home.

"Are you alright?" Chi Chi asked tilting her head towards me.

"Yes I just feel like something in my life is about to change."

As I pulled up in front of my garage, my cell phone rang. I couldn't figure out who would be calling me at 2am.

"Hello? This is Jada."

The voice on the other side sounding like Barry White said, "this is Maliek. I was calling to see if you made it home safely."

"Yes I just pulled in."

"Do you see a white escalade truck passing by?"

"Yes I do."

"Don't be alarmed, that's Ali, one of my bodyguards just making sure you got home safe."

"Wow I really don't know what to say. Thank you."

"Not a problem, just making sure."

"When will I get a chance to meet you?" I asked

"I'll get with you as soon as I can clear up some time off my calendar. I'll call you."

"Ok, good night."

I held on to my phone after he hung up, and of course Chi Chi was waiting in her seat impatiently. She knew it was him. I just screamed.

"Yes, he called me. It's about to go down."

We got out of the car and went into the house. We said our goodnights and went into our separate bedrooms ready to crash after such an adventurous evening. As I got into my king-sized canopy bed with satin sheets, I grabbed the magazine that had his picture in it and I held it close to my heart. I knew God was looking out for me. I said a prayer and drifted off to sleep.

CHAPTER 8

Morning came so fast, and the next thing I heard was my alarm. I had forgotten it was Saturday. I decided to have a personal day to get my hair done, a manicure, pedicure and just do a little shopping. I got out of bed, took a shower, put on some jogging pants and put my hair back in a clip. I decided not to disturb Chi Chi, knowing that she needed all the rest she could get.

I first went to the hair salon to get my hair done, then the nail salon, then on to the Fairlane Mall, which was just around the corner from the nail salon. I got some new outfits, even though I didn't really need to buy any; but I figured since I was going to be dating, I needed to get some sexy pieces that I didn't have. I was now ready for Mr. Montana. I was more than set for him. As I drove home from the mall I called Chi Chi to see if she needed anything while I was out.

She wondered why I didn't wake her up to join me since she would have loved to spend some money, but I knew she needed her beauty rest, and knew how irate she got when abruptly disturbed. She asked me to pick up a movie we could watch later.

While driving, I listened to Gerald Levert's CD called *My Songs*. I missed him already but I had enough of his music to keep him alive forever. When I got back home, I decided to unwind by soaking in the tub with my lavender-scented candles. Oh how relaxing it was. My mom called me just as I was getting out of the tub.

"Hello mom, how are you doing?"

"Fine baby, I was just calling to see if my baby girl was going to give God some praise on Sunday."

"Ma, I think I am going to make it."

We talked for a little while. My mom made it a habit to call me during the week or on Saturdays to remind me to go to church on Sundays. She would always tell me to get my praise on and to not forget who kept me alive daily. I guess I was still a little girl in her eyes.

After Chi Chi and I sat and talked and watched a couple of movies, it was time to get ready for a night out. I chose to wear a diamond pendent and a matching tennis bracelet with a beautiful Chanel spaghetti strapped dress and silver stilettos. Meanwhile, Chi Chi was all dressed up. She would usually wear something with jeans but not tonight. This time she wore a shimmering skirt with a matching top and brown stiletto boots. She looked like she was going to an engagement party. After I was done dressing, I admired myself in the mirror, and Chi Chi's phone rang.

"Jada, I'm going to see you later."

I thought it strange that her date did not come to the door to get her. My mom would have had a fit if my date didn't come to the door, or if he was the type of man that just blows his horn if he was taking me on a date. Chi Chi called me on her cell phone when she was in the car and whispered," don't give the goods on the first date."And then with a loud voice she said, "I forgot to tell you to have fun."

"Yeah. You too, have fun."

The doorbell rang, and I opened to find a limo driver standing there.

"I am here to escort you to the Club Stallion."

"Ok I will be right out."

I checked myself in the mirror one last time to make sure everything was fine and walked out of the house proudly. The driver stood by the wide open door of the limo, and I got in. *Now this is what I am talking about,* said to myself as he closed the door.

We then proceeded to the club and I was looking out the window like a celebrity, amazed at how I was being pampered. When we got to the club, the driver didn't pull into the front entrance but to a side entrance I had never noticed. There was a young man dressed in an Armani suit that came and opened my door.

"Good evening," He said

"Good evening."

This side of the club was totally different. It was nothing I would have ever imagined.

"Follow me please," He said.

He then stuck his key card in the entrance door and we stepped inside. There were beautiful plants in an atrium glass that ran all the way to the ceiling. It was magnificent. The room was overlaid with gold trimmings. This place was fit for royalty. I followed the gentleman to the elevator and he used his keycard to take me to the third floor. When the doors swung open, there stood a tall, dark-skinned man with hazel eyes, short wavy hair and broad shoulders in a tailored suit. He carefully took my right hand and kissed it. I instantly blushed.

"Hello Jada, I am Maliek Montana."

"It is a pleasure to meet you," I said as my legs weakened at the sight of this gorgeous man.

"The pleasure is all mine," He said.

The whole room was immaculately decorated. A table for two had been set up in the middle of the room; and on the right, there was a baby grand white piano. It looked like something straight out of a magazine. I felt really special. A few minutes later, a gentleman in a black tuxedo walked over to the piano and started playing some of my favorite love songs. Maliek was still holding my hand as we walked to the table. He pulled my chair out for me to sit and made sure I was comfortable before he took his seat.

"Why thank you," I said with my eyes glued to his face.

This man was a gentleman. A man is not a man until he can be a gentleman. I didn't know how to act around him because he had class and etiquette. His chef walked into the room and introduced himself as Sung. Sung had been Maliek's personal chef for a very long time.

"I brought him here especially for you," He said, staring right into my eyes.

"That's very thoughtful of you," I said, not knowing how much of this I could take.

A waiter come up to the table with a bottle of Don Perigon and poured it into our champagne glasses.

"Here's to you and me getting to know each other better."

"I'll drink to that," I said.

After my first sip, I relaxed. The whole event was too perfect. Sung rolled a fabulous meal over to the table. Our first course was hors d'oeuvres. Then our second course was a salad that was scrumptious. For our main course, we had lobster with potatoes, broccoli and cheese sauce. It was well laid out. We started talking about our present life situations and what we were both looking for in a relationship. He couldn't believe I was not dating anyone. I asked him if he was and he said he wasn't in any serious relationship.

"Don't get me wrong, I do have my needs, but it's coming to a point in my life where I want to take things more seriously."

We realized we had a lot in common and we got more and more comfortable with each other. The more we talked, the more we laughed and enjoyed each other's company. Just then, the piano player began to play a collection of Luther Vandross songs. Maliek asked me to dance and I agreed. He could really dance and carry a beat, and I was in heaven in his arms. Watching him dance made me realize that I wanted to be with this man.

The pianist played Keith Sweat's song, "In The Rain" and this time I grabbed Maliek and we began to grind. I could feel his manhood rising. We danced until 2am. This was one of the most wonderful nights I had ever had in my entire life. It was a new thing for me. I didn't know any young men who could treat you like a queen. I thought that only older men were capable, but I learned something new that day.

After the last song played, we held each other for a while. Then I said, "I think I am ready to retire for the night."

"Me too. It's funny how time flies when you are having a good time."

I had even forgotten that it was my Saturday to work. We decided to leave and this time Maliek accompanied me. Once we got into the limo, he took my hand into his.

"Can we see each other again?"

"Yes I would like that." I was already feeling safe with him and I knew that he was the man I wanted to be with. We reached my condo and he walked me to my door.

"Maliek, I had a wonderful time tonight."

"So did I."

He pulled me into his arms and kissed me very deeply and passionately as though there was no tomorrow. After we caught our breath, we stared into each other's eyes for a minute before we said goodnight. I opened my door and he started to walk towards the Limo. He kept looking back shaking his head in amazement and we waved goodbye to each other. He waited for me to get into the house, before his limo driver drove off.

CHAPTER 9

Monday started off just fine. We had a really busy morning. I was sitting at my desk at about 10:30a.m., when I looked up to see a fine man walking through the door. He was 6ft tall, dark skinned, light brown eyes, and wore a black and white pin stripped suit with a long jacket. He also sported some black and white Stacy Adams shoes. You could smell his cologne from the time he walked into the bank. I could see he was asking the security guard Mr. Hall where he could go to open up a new account. Mr. Hall pointed him to my direction. He approached my desk.

"May I help you?"

In a deep voice he replied, "Yes, I would like to open up a new account."

"Alright sir, please have a seat."

He sat down on the brown leather chair that was right across from my desk. I asked him if this was his first time opening an account here and it was. I asked him for is identification card, and he handed it to me. It read, Reverend James Turner III.

"How much will you be depositing today sir?"

"One million dollars Ms. James," he said, as he read my name off the placard that was on my desk.

"Oh Mr. Turner, I see you are a minister."

"Yes I am. Do you attend church?"

"Yes. I have been going to Community COGIC, but I haven't made it my church home as of yet."

"I feel ya. But don't wait too long."

After I finished up with his application, I had him sign it and he handed me his check.

"I am inviting you to come and visit with us," He said as he passed me one of his business cards.

"That pastor Trellis can really preach. I have known him as an acquaintance for quite some time."

"Thank you I will keep that in mind."

"Have a nice day and God bless you," He said.

"You too Sir."

He got up and left. His cologne continued to permeate the room and lingered most of the day. That was one of the finest preachers I had ever seen. He dressed well and was also young. He could have easily been mistaken for something else. He may have been married, but I didn't see him wearing a wedding band. I assumed he was single.

I resumed my work and debated about whether I would go to the gym after work or go home and relax. I was still a little tired from the weekend. Eventually, I decided to go home and relax. I also looked forward to hearing from Maliek.

As I got ready to leave work, Mr. Hall, walked up to me.

"Ms. James, let me walk you out."

"Thank you Mr. Hall, that is very generous of you."

"It's my job young lady and I enjoy looking out for you all."

After I got home, I changed into some sweats and logged onto my laptop. As I was browsing on Google, Chi Chi came home. We talked about how our days went and I told her about Reverend Turner. My cell rang about 8:30pm. It was none other than Maliek.

"Hello, this is Jada."

"How are you?"

"I'm fine and yourself?"

"I'm doing good," He said in his deep voice. His voice was driving me crazy.

"Jada, I was wondering if you would like to come down to the club on Friday?"

"Sure," I said excitedly.

"You don't have to drive. I will have my limo driver pick you up at around 8:00pm, if that's good with you?"

"Yes that will be fine."

"It's a date."

"Yes it is."

There was a silence on the phone. It seemed we were both at a loss for words.

"Are you still there?" He said

"Yes I'm still here. I will see you Friday ok?"

"Good. See you then."

We hang up the phone and I screamed Chi Chi's name as I ran into her room, only to find her on her phone. I jumped on her bed with a huge smile on my face as I waited for her to finish with her call. After she hung up, we both looked at each other and fell back on the bed laughing. Chi Chi said, "let me hear your news first."

"Ok. Maliek and I have a date on Friday. Now tell me who you were talking to."

She started moving her head from side to side as if to make me wait longer for her response, and then she busted out saying

"It was CJ. I'm going out with him on Friday too."

"Girl for real? Why do you seem as though you are not excited?"

"Well, why can't I meet a guy like Maliek?"

"Well, you never know what may come out of your date, until you go for your date. I am happy for you though."

"Ok Jada, but you know how I am with relationships and I don't really trust men like you."

"Chi Chi, It's not that I trust men, the truth is that I just don't want to be left alone. I am also not after Maliek's money. I just need some happiness in my life and someone to love me back."

"Yeah me too." She hugged me. We then started to sing the song "Just got paid . . . Friday night."

We talked about what we were going to wear until it was time to turn in.

CHAPTER 10

Friday didn't come fast enough. Every evening after I got home, I went to bed earlier than usual, and during the week, I only got to go to the gym twice. I worked until 1:00pm, since I had an appointment with my hairstylist. My hairstylist's name was Deborah. She worked at the Monique's Monea Hair Salon. When I walked into the shop, it was very crowded. She'd changed my appointment from Saturday to Friday as a favor.

"Girl you better be glad you one of my favorite customers. Now sit your butt right here," she said as she pointed to the now empty chair, since she had made another customer switch seats. The customer rolled her eyes at me. Deb was flat ironing my hair when she said, "girl you look so happy. What's up with you? What's your secret?"

"I will tell you all about it later."

She continued to flat iron my hair while I reminisced about my ex-boyfriend and how after MSU he transferred to Harvard University, where he soon after started dating another girl. I thought about how he would tell me sweet nothings and give me empty promises of how I was the only girl for him and that there was never going to be anyone for him but me. But I knew deep down he was not truthful. I found out the hard way. One day I decided to give him a surprise visit only to realize his betrayal. He broke my heart. So I vowed never to let any man close to me like that again. Deb spun the chair around so I could see from the hand mirror if the hair was good. My hair was not only bouncy, but stylish. I was very impressed.

"Girl, you know you are bad," I said to her.

"Yeah that's coz I make most of my money off you. Just look how many customers you have sent me this past year."

"Yeah that's right, and I will continue to send them to you."

I paid her and also gave her a twenty dollar tip. It was time to head home, but not without fighting through traffic. When I got home, I found Chi Chi all dressed up and glowing.

"What's with the glow?" I asked.

She was really excited about her date but nobody could beat my excitement.

"Jada, do you know how long it's been since I've been on a date?"

"I am your best friend, or have you forgotten?" I said.

"Has CJ told you where he is taking you?"

"No, He said it is a surprise."

"You go girl. Have a good time."

"You too."

CHAPTER 11

Maliek told his driver to drive him to his mansion. He could not stop thinking about Jada and how fine and lovely she was. He knew that it would take some time to break down the wall she had built up but it was a step he was willing to take. He enjoyed the experience he had with her. It was very special to him, especially after he had dated so many women. There was something special about Jada. She didn't know it but she had him smiling and laughing. This was something that had not happened to him in quite some time.

He had been business only lately. He did go on casual dates from time to time, which he really dreaded, because most of the women were just after his money and sex. He had come to a point in his life where he wanted love and he wanted it bad. He thought he had found someone he could love and give the world. Jada had already let him know she wasn't looking for money but for someone to love and to love her back. He couldn't get her out of his mind.

When I was in my foyer, I stood against the door with my eyes closed, reminiscing about the last embrace Maliek and I shared. When I opened my eyes, I saw Chi Chi sitting on the sofa crying her eyes out. I quickly came out of my daze and rushed over and sat by her

"What's the matter?"

"My date turned out to be a disaster!"

"Stop crying and tell me what happened." I put my purse on the table and went into the bathroom to get her a wet towel, and then put my arm around her.

"CJ is a maniac," she said.

"What do you mean he is a maniac?"

"Well he took me to his house and we had a nice dinner. After dinner we sat on the couch with our drinks. I had some wine while he had Jack Daniels and you know he was really killing it. After he had enough, he started feeling it and so he tried to force himself on me. I kept telling him to stop and trying to move away from him, but he kept coming on to me trying to take my clothes off. He said that he thought I wanted him bad and that I was sitting all up in the club enticing him and showing him my goods, which was a lie. I know I was not indecent at the club, and I never thought I was leading him on. If anything, he was the one that was flirting with me. You saw the way he was all on me in the club.

"Tell me what happened next."

"He straddled me on the couch and tore off my blouse then tried to get the rest of my clothes off saying 'you women think you can go around teasing men all the time half-dressed and flirting.' He unzipped his pants and exposed himself and starting massaging himself. I guess he thought I would give in once I saw what was in his pants. Instead, I found some strength and managed to push him off me. He fell to the floor, I grabbed my purse and dashed out of the house. It just so happened that there was a cab passing through his neighborhood. That's how I got home. I even left my shoes at his house."

"Why did you take your shoes off?"

"Because when I got there I was relaxed and I was really feeling him. He even gave me a foot massage before he got drunk."

"Oh girl, I am so sorry that he was a monster. Do you want me to call the police?"

"No I just want to take a bath and go to bed."

I hugged her. She got up and went into the bathroom. I felt really bad for her. CJ didn't appear to be the kind of man that would do what he did. Though, I did have a strange feeling about him earlier not coming to the door to get her when he picked her up for their date. I went to bedroom and dialed Maliek's number. Unfortunately, it went straight to voicemail. I assumed he had already gone to sleep.

CHAPTER 12

I had a hard time sleeping that night. Finally about an hour before my usual wake up time, I decided to go jogging for half an hour. I needed to relive some of the stress. *If only I could have picked him out and warned her.* I really thought he was a nice man, but I was wrong and now my best friend had to suffer another scar. After I ran five miles, I decided to go back home and get ready for work. I checked on Chi Chi before leaving but she was still asleep. I wrote her a note saying that if she needed me to call me, and that I would come home immediately.

As soon as I got into my car, my phone rang. It was Maliek.

"I see you tried to call me last night. I'm sorry I didn't answer, but I was already asleep."

"I was calling you to tell you about your little bartender."

"Yeah? What about him?"

"He took my friend Chi Chi, the one that came to the club with me, on a date last night and after he got her into his house, he started drinking and tried to rape her."

"What now Jada? Slow down and run that by me again!"

I narrated the story all over again to him.

"I don't believe this. Jada I am so sorry that this happened. It's a great shock to me. I never would have imagined that anyone I know and that works for me would have the audacity to pull a stunt like that that. Is she ok?"

"Yes when I left home she was still sleeping."

I could tell by his voice he was very upset and disappointed.

"Could I please have Chi Chi's number? I would like to give her a call personally and apologize to her. You better believe I am going to handle this and I will call you later. Again, I am sorry."

I gave him the number and we hang up.

As I drove to work, I thought again about CJ's behavior and how he couldn't even come to the door when he picked up Chi Chi for their date. I also thought about my relationship with Maliek and I hoped that this incident would not affect our relationship even though I knew he was nothing like CJ.

When I got to work, I was glad to know I would only be there half the day. That way, I would get to spend the rest of the day with my friend. After work, I stopped by Blockbuster and picked up a couple of Tyler Perry movies. I figured we needed something funny to brighten up the day. As I waited to pay for the movies, Maliek called me and I got a tingle all over my body.

"Hello baby, how are you doing?"

"I am good. I am here at Blockbuster picking up some movies "I was calling to see if you and Chi Chi were ok. I do apologize again for CJ's behavior. I must tell you that I have never seen this side of CJ before. I guess it's because I don't allow any of my employees to drink on the job. Nevertheless, I do pay attention to my employees. Had I known he was a Dr. Jekyl, this problem would have been resolved a long time ago. I run a good and respectful business and I don't need anyone bringing heat around me. I tried calling Chi Chi earlier but I think she was still asleep, but I will try her again as soon as I finish talking to you."

"You're right. She was probably still sleeping."

"Jada, I hope you don't have any bad thoughts about me because of CJ?"

My heart flipped. "No Maliek, I don't. I know you are not like him."

"Ok baby, I will talk to you later."

"Ok. I said and we hung up."

I left the video store and hopped in my car. Maliek Montana dominated my thoughts once again.

CHAPTER 13

I stopped at the gas station to fill up my car like I do every Saturday. It normally lasts me the entire week. As I stood there pumping, I heard a deep voice come up behind me.

"Can I help you pump that gas young lady?"

"Oh, hi Reverend Turner. Why sure you can."

I could smell that same cologne I had smelled in my office the day he'd walked in. He had his Lincoln Navigator running nearby.

"It's good to see you again Ms. James."

"Yeah, you too Rev. What are you doing on this side of town?"

"Oh, just getting gas. It's never that busy and I enjoy the ride over here. On top of that, the gas is better. My vehicles seem to run smoother on the gas from this place."

"I agree with you 100%. "And I really appreciate this."

"Not a problem," he said as he finished pumping.

I starting walking inside to pay the attendant.

"Rev., I'm looking forward to visiting your church. I can't say exactly when, but I'll be there."

"Ok, the doors are always open," he said as he jumped into his truck and pulled off.

When I returned to my car, I could still smell his cologne. *That is one fine man,* I thought to myself. Upon arriving home, the aroma of fried chicken greeted me. Chi Chi was frying some wings and homemade french fries. I should have known this would happen because whenever she gets upset she loves to cook and eat. I walked over to the stove where she was standing.

"Girl, you are really doin' it!"

"Yeah, I need to get some of this stress off me"

I washed my hands in the sink.

"Girl, we can talk about that later. I'm starving."

I fixed my plate and sat on one of the barstools.

"So, Chi Chi, how you doing?"

"Jada, I'm trying to figure out if what just happened to me was a dream or reality. Maliek called me to express his feelings and asked me if he could do anything for me. I assured him that it wasn't his fault and thanked him for being concerned. He also told me not to let that stop me from coming to his club, and that when I do come, I would never have to pay for anything."

I could see that my soon-to-be man was very thoughtful.

"Girl, I never did get a chance to tell you, we really had a good time the other night. I haven't had that type of treatment ever in my life. He is such a gentleman. And girl, fine on top of fine!"

My facial expression started to get dreamy.

"Chi Chi, why are you looking at me like that? I know where your mind is. No, we didn't cross the line, so don't even ask. You know I'm old-fashioned. Definitely nothing happening on the first date."

"Girl, CJ probably would have gotten some from me if he hadn't tried to force himself on me. You know I was horny too. What a waste, as fine as he was. You have to be careful nowadays going out with these men you think are all that, especially going to their house real fast. The next time I go on a date, it will be in a public place, maybe even a football stadium."

"It's good to see you laugh Chi Chi. And being your best friend I really hope you will find someone to make you happy. I wish you could have heard the pastor last Sunday talking about waiting on the Lord. He also said that it could apply to many areas of our lives."

"I'll keep that in mind. You know Jada, maybe I'm looking for love in all the wrong places. I'm seriously thinking about going back to Atlanta for a while. My parents will love that, and I'm long overdue for some pampering."

"Yeah, I agree. I would really hate to see you leave me, but if that will make you feel better, I'm with you. Just don't stay too long. We can fly to see each other."

"And Chi Chi, this food is so good. Your southern touch hasn't left you. Maybe we can find a lot to do before you leave. Don't forget, we haven't gone skating in a long time.

I pretended to skate in the middle of the floor. Chi Chi cracked up when I stomped. I realized how full and sleepy I was at the same time.

"Chi Chi I bought some movies but I want to shower and lay down for while."

"That's ok, girl. I can watch Tyler Perry all by my lonesome."

I gave her the bag and headed to my room.

CHAPTER 14

I went to work all refreshed on Monday, because Sunday, Chi Chi and I cooked, ate and watched movies. Although I was really happy to see she was moving on after CJ's foolishness, I was even happier that Maliek had stopped by to see if we were ok. *What a man!*

When he walked through the door all iced out, I just melted. Before he left, he grabbed me around my waist, and I thought I would faint. He gave me a kiss that made me want to walk him to my bedroom and give him something he had never had. But it was much too early for any of that.

I glanced up at my clock while I was sitting at my desk doing reports on my computer and saw that it was exactly 9:00a.m. Right at that moment, a delivery boy walked into the bank. I saw him talk to the security guard, Mr. Hall, who pointed him towards my office. The delivery guy then walked through my door.

He had me sign for delivery of six yellow roses, six white roses and twelve red roses. There was also a card that read "My limo will pick you up at 7pm." I was completely illuminated with excitement! All I could do was smile and take long deep breaths as I floated away in emotional bliss. Soon, some of the other tellers came into my office complimenting me and telling me how beautiful the flowers made my office look.

After all the excitement died down, I turned my computer off and went to a staff meeting. I hated staff meetings because they were so boring and repetitive. Plus my mind wasn't on work at this point anyway. When the meeting was over, I walked across the street to the deli to grab some lunch. I sat down at the table and called Maliek. He answered on the first ring.

"Maliek, you are so full of surprises. I love the roses you sent, and the poem. I'm looking forward to seeing you tonight."

"Well, you haven't seen the other surprises that I have for you. This only happens when someone like yourself catches my eye. There are no limits. I'm glad you like the flowers and I'll see you tonight."

I went back to the counter to pick up my sandwich and daydreamed about Maliek. Everything seemed so surreal. I finished my lunch and went back to work, hoping the remainder of the day would pass quickly.

I left work and stopped by the nail shop on my way home to get my red polished retouched. When I got home, I rummaged through my closet trying to decide what I was going to wear. I settled on red outfit I'd been dying to wear for quite some time. Then I took a soothing bath in some wonderfully scented strawberries and cream oil that did wonders for my skin.

Chi Chi wasn't at home, so I figured she must have stopped at the gym to work out. I got dressed but my hair was kind of acting up so I pinned it up and it turned out really well with the outfit I wore.

Maliek was so full of surprises that I could only imagine what he had planned for the night. I wrote Chi Chi a note before I left, to let her know my whereabouts since I rarely went out during the week.

My limo came at exactly 7 o'clock. We drove around for about 30 minutes and the ride seemed like it went on forever. Eventually, the driver turned down a long driveway. I saw a huge swimming pool, sauna, tennis court, basketball court and what looked like a mini football field. I also saw several guest houses. When we approached the entrance, along the top of the electronic gate was written in fancy letters *Montana Estates*.

Once the gates swung open, I could see the front of the mansion. It was magnificent! The limo drove to the front of the house and Maliek was standing there waiting to greet me in a two-piece Versace suit with matching shoes. His eyes were glued to me from the time the driver opened my door. He kissed me and grabbed my hand.

"Welcome to my home," he said, as he led me into his mansion.

His house was decorated with black and white marble. The furnishings were white with gold accents.

"Let me give you a tour," he said.

"You mean to tell me you live here alone?" I said in disbelief.

"Yes," he said.

He led me through nine bedrooms, five of which had Jacuzzi tubs. The master suite had a bathtub that seemed like it was half the size of a small swimming pool. There was also a pool room, movie theater, an enormous dining room, a study, a family room which had a wall to wall aquarium, two sunken dens, two kitchens, and a twelve-car garage. There were also four guest houses, two of which were occupied by the maid and chef.

"Why haven't you ever been married, Maliek?"

"Well, Jada, because I just haven't found anyone that I thought was worthy of being my wife. Most of the ladies I have encountered loved material things and really had no desire to love me. I have everything I could ever want and more. This was my goal to reach before I reached age 35. So, I'm basically looking for someone to share all that I have."

He looked at me as if he were looking at my soul. I walked over and ran my fingers across his collection of movies. He continued to stare at me. We selected one to watch after dinner.

We ate outside on the terrace and the food was wonderful. Amidst our talking and laughing, Maliek walked around the table and grabbed my hand again.

"Are you ready to go to the movies?" he said.

As soon as I stood up, he grabbed me around my waist and began stroking the side of my face. Before I knew it, he was cradling the back of my head and we were locked into a passionate kiss. We were lost in each other for a moment, and I definitely didn't want to be found. I was really feeling this man. I just couldn't believe that all of this was true.

We stood on the terrace holding one another and staring into one another's eyes.

"Do you think we can try to make something out of this?" he said. "You don't have to answer me right now."

"Yes I do," I answered with virtually no hesitation, as he hugged me tighter.

"I guess this makes it official," he said. "You are now my woman and I'm your man."

We continued to embrace and shared more passionate kisses for a while longer. I knew he wanted to ask me to stay the night but I couldn't do it.

We decided not to watch a movie, but went into the den to talk more and get to know each other even better. We were having so much fun and the hours were flying by. I didn't want the night to end but I knew it was time for me to go. We rode in the limo back to my house and I sat snuggled against him as we held hands. I knew that Maliek and I would now be virtually inseparable. The limo pulled up to my condo and we both got out.

He walked me to the my front door, and as soon as I pulled my key out, he gently took it from my hand, unlocked and opened the door for me.

"Now you belong to Maliek and you have no more worries in this world," he said.

We kissed once more and said our goodnights. When Chi Chi heard the door close, she came out of the dining room to greet me.

"Girl, come here and let me take a good look at you to see if you've done the thang!"

"Not yet Chi Chi," I said. "But come in my room while I get comfortable and let me tell you about this man's house."

Chi Chi followed me into my room all excited to hear.

I described to her everything that I'd seen that night and told her how hard it was to believe that this was really happening. We agreed that it was almost a fairytale-like experience. After I'd given her all the details and sat on my bed, I could tell something was on Chi Chi's mind.

"Jada, I've made up my mind that I'm leaving in a week, but look how things have worked out for you. You have a new man, so you won't be lonesome. That was something I was concerned about, but I'm so glad that everything is gonna be way better than I expected."

Chi Chi's decision to leave still hurt me, but I didn't let her see how sad I was to hear that she was leaving in a week. Despite my new-found happiness, I still was going to miss her terribly. But reminded myself to focus on my new life with my new man.

CHAPTER 15

The past week was the greatest I'd had in a while. Chi Chi and I had gone skating, eating, shopping and just having a good time together. Maliek left the club a couple of nights and stopped by to hang out with us.

His continual presence was a healing of sorts to me, because the void I had so long felt was virtually gone now. I was loving every moment of now having someone in my life who cared about me deeply and went out of their way to show it.

Sunday morning came and I was debating about whether I wanted to go to church or not. I got up and knocked on Chi Chi's door to see if she wanted to go. She agreed that we should. We both showered and grabbed a light breakfast before heading out.

We decided to go to Rev. Turner's church, and arrived during the prayer session. We took a seat in the middle aisle and he came out to the podium just as we got settled.

"Girl, is that the preacher with the best smelling cologne in the world you were talking about?" Chi Chi said.

I confirmed that it was him, just as Rev. Turner noticed us in the congregation and gave us an acknowledging nod. His message was called "It's A Set Up," and he talked about how the devil will trick you into different things to set you up for a fall, then laugh at you. Chi Chi and I cried throughout the entire service. It was so impactful to me because I could relate to everything he talked about. I guess it hit a lot of people, because they were praising the Lord all over the church.

After service, we made our way down to the front to shake the pastor's hand but it was hard to get to him because there were so many sisters swarming around him, competing for his attention. When it was our turn, I introduced he and Chi Chi to one another. Rev. Turner extended his hand to her.

"I'm so glad you young ladies made it to our service today. Did you enjoy the service?"

"We loved it," we said in unison.

"Well, don't let this be your last time," he said.

We walked outside and got in the car. Chi Chi looked at me.

"Girl, I can see that man makes large deposits in the bank. Look at that congregation. You sure he's a preacher? If I met him in the streets, I wouldn't believe he was a preacher because of how fine he is. How long he been preachin'?"

"I don't know Chi Chi. But I believe he's a true man of God. You can tell he had some type of street life before. That goes to show that God can change anyone."

"I would have tried to get with him if it wasn't in church," Chi Chi said.

"Girl, stop," I said.

"That man used to be big time. Just the air about him," she said.

We drove to Steve's Soul Food and went inside to eat instead of carrying it out. While we were waiting on the waitress to bring our food, Chi Chi and I discussed how much we were going to miss one another. We were best friends, and were really more like sisters. We decided that we'd hang out at Maliek's club that coming Friday as one of our last outings before she left. We finished eating and talking, paid for our food and left a tip on the table.

We were so full when we got home that all we could do was shower, change clothes and relax. We watched a Tyler Perry movie and laughed until we were in tears. My phone rang in the middle of the movie. It was Maliek.

"How's my favorite girl doing," he said.

"Fine. How are you?" I asked.

"I'm good. What you up to?" he said.

"Watching *Madea* with Chi Chi," I said. "We went to church this morning."

"Oh good," he said. "Did you say a prayer for me?"

"You know I did," I said. "How could I leave you out?"

We laughed a little. I told Maliek about Chi Chi going back to Atlanta and how we were going to miss each other, but that Chi Chi needed a little vacation from things. I also told him how we planned to come to his club on Friday before she left.

"Oh good," Maliek said. "Would you like me to set up something for her? And speaking of vacations, I was actually calling to tell you that I wanted to take you to St. Thomas to one of my resorts. But we'll talk about that. In the meantime though, we'll do something special for Chi Chi. He then told me that I didn't need to pack too much and that he wanted to take me shopping.

"I'm at a loss for words," I said. "I don't know what to say."

"Don't say anything," he replied. "Just comply with my request."

"You already know my answer is yes," I said.

"Ok, it's set then," he said.

We blew phone kisses and said goodbye.

"Don't tell me you're going to St. Thomas," Chi Chi said after I shared the news.

"Yes girl – I sure am," I said. "And I guess you know it's about to go down."

"I'm so happy for you," Chi Chi said. "You landed a man that has it going on, and I'm sure you will call me and tell me all about it."

"You got that right," I said. "He'll be my Romeo for sure after this. I've got to get in the bed Chi Chi, and so do you. Good night girl."

CHAPTER 16

I loved my job. The security officer, Mr. Hall, made everyone smile when they came into the bank. He'd been working there forever. I walked through the door well-dressed as usual, and was greeted by Mr. Hall's smiling face.

"Good morning Ms. James."

Mr. Hall would always rehearse the same little story with me about the bank. He'd always say, "they can rob us, just as long as the women are as fine as the ones in *Set It Off*, and are wearing bikinis." We'd always laugh at this ridiculous scenario and I'd continue to my office.

This was going to be an exciting week and one of great change. The trip to St. Thomas with Maliek dominated my thoughts. After working the first part of the morning, just before I could wrap up for lunch, a young man walked into my office unannounced and handed me a box with a bow on top.

"Compliments of Maliek," he said. He then walked away.

I opened the box and noticed that there was a smaller box inside. I opened the smaller one and there were five-carat diamond earrings inside. *Lord, what kind of man do I have*, I thought to myself. I tried calling Maliek but kept getting his voicemail, so I left him a message: *"baby, I received your lovely gift and thank you so much. You truly have a way of brightening up my day."*

In examining the earrings closer, I concluded that he must have paid quite a bit for them, and that money must never be an issue for him. As the day came to a close, I went to see my boss to let him know that I wouldn't be coming in on Monday. He told me that it wouldn't be a problem, especially since I was one of his employees that never took days off.

On my way home, just as I was pulling in, Maliek called me and told me he had gotten my message and that he would do anything for his new baby. He also asked me to invite some more of our friends for Friday. I asked him what he was up to, but of course he wouldn't share any more details. He only guaranteed that everything was going to be "hot" and something we'd never forget.

I got a little sad when he told me he would be out of town for a few days before Friday, but assured me that he'd be back in plenty of time. He also told me that the limo would be coming to pick us up at 6:30pm. I hung up, and went to the work out center. The usual bunch was there, but I wasn't being flirtatious like I normally would.

This bodybuilder named Sky was walking towards us. *Uh oh.* I was tying my gym shoes and he stood in from of me. He was quite chiseled. He was standing so close, but this was supposedly his way of "getting his rap on."

"What's up Jada?" he said.

I sat straight up. "Oh, nothing," I said. "Getting ready to sweat a little."

"I thought you were going to give me a call so that we could go out," he said.

"Sky, I never promised you anything," I said. "I told you I don't go out that much."

"Oh, so now what? You telling me you got a man now?"

"As a matter of fact I do," I said, as I stood up.

"You should have told me, so I wouldn't be wasting my precious time, trying to get with you," he said.

I didn't reply and left him standing there looking like a oversized incredible hulk. After one hour of doing my normal workout, I went in, took a shower and got dressed. As I was leaving, Sky was kneeled in front of a new chick, massaging her ankle. *Thank God he's got somebody else to bother*, I thought to myself.

He and I smiled at each other. Sky thought his body could capture any woman. The problem was, his body was all he had to offer – his conversation was horrible.

I drove home and started helping Chi Chi pack some of her clothes.

"Girl, so how do you feel about your romantic getaway?" she said.

"I am so excited and nervous," I said. "This is the first time we are going to spend the night together."

"Jada, just take a little at a time," she said. "I wish you the best and hope things work out. I never want to see you hurt again and it seems like Maliek is a good man. Sometimes we fall into situations and really don't know what the outcome is gonna be."

"You're right about that," I said. "I'm going to take it slow, and since tomorrow is Friday, I'm going to take a half day, so I can get ready for the whole weekend."

"I'm not going at all," she said while taping up her last box. "My boss gave me an extended leave of absence, so that I can come back at any time."

CHAPTER 17

Friday morning arrived and I had so much to do. I got off work and went to get my hair done, then paid some bills, and did some shopping. It was around 4 o'clock when I finished doing that, so I still had plenty of time to get dressed. I was so excited about seeing Maliek.

Chi Chi and I decided get totally dolled up, wearing Gucci from head to toe. We looked like we were headed to a professional video shoot. The limo driver rang the doorbell. He was always prompt, a total gentleman and the consummate professional. He drove us to the club and Maliek came out to escort us inside.

After giving me a kiss and hugging Chi Chi, he told us that we had about 20 guests already waiting for us.

"Where are they?" I said.

"I know you didn't think I wanted my number one girl and her going away friend to party on the first floor," said Maliek.

We got on the elevator and rode to the third floor. Then we walked to the end of the hallway and Maliek opened the door to one of the private rooms.

"SURPISE CHI CHI!" everyone screamed.

The party was already crunk and people were dancing everywhere. The room was decorated in black and white, with gold balloons everywhere. There was also a fountain in the middle of the floor, bubbling forth only the finest champagne. In addition to the guests we'd invited, Maliek had also invited some NBA and NFL players, and other high profile people.

Chi Chi hugged Maliek and giddily thanked him for orchestrating such an incredible party.

"You're welcome," he said. "Anything for my baby," he said, as he wrapped one arm around my waist.

Maliek then walked over to the DJ and picked up the microphone.

"All the men will have to leave at 10 o'clock, but for now, everyone hit the floor and let's cha cha!" he said.

When time came, all the men reluctantly started leaving but complied with Maliek's directions. Chi Chi was still sitting conversing with one the gentlemen she'd met. The lights in the club slowly began to dim and the DJ played Maxwell's "A Woman's Work." Things got a bit wild when 10 male exotic dancers made their entrance into the place. All the ladies shrieked and covered their mouths in disbelief.

At the end of the song, the balloons burst open and money started raining from the ceiling.

"Jada, your man really knows how to throw a party," Chi Chi said.

"Yeah, he is something," I said.

I was smiling from ear to ear. This was truly a night to remember.

CHAPTER 18

When morning came, it seemed as if I had just lay down. All night long I kept waking up, unable to sleep. I guess I was so excited about spending the weekend with Maliek. As soon as my clock sounded at 6:00 a.m., I jumped out bed, took my shower and got dressed. Maliek arrived at 7 and rung the doorbell. I was standing in Chi Chi's doorway. She was so tired from the night before that she didn't even respond when I first called her.

"Good morning sweetheart," Maliek said, as he kissed me on the lips.

"When you say early, you really mean early," I said.

"Yes," he said. "I felt like we needed to get an early start since we are only staying over the weekend. Where is Chi Chi?"

"Where else?" I said. "After that party you gave her, she's still in the bed."

"Hey Maliek," Chi Chi hollered through the door.

"Hey – we're leaving now," he said, as he walked out to the car.

I locked the door to my place and looked up to find him standing next to a black Ferrari. We drove outside the city to a private airstrip. A gentleman came to Maliek's side of the car to let Maliek know that his jet was fueled and ready to go. We parked the car in a garage and walked over to the jet that was a few hundred yards away.

I could barely believe my eyes, as I took in the image of a white Learjet that had "Montana #1" written on the side of it. Maliek's face of full of joy and satisfaction. He could tell that my excitement and surprise were barely containable.

The inside of the jet was immaculate and spacious, with room for 8 people. Everything was beautiful white leather and smelled brand new. The pilot came over the intercom: *Mr. Montana, as soon as you all get seated and you give me the ok, we'll be ready for takeoff.*

"Jada, do you want something to drink to relax your nerves before we take off?" Maliek said.

"Yes," I said, and Maliek fixed a drink on the rocks for each of us.

He fastened my seatbelt, then seated and secured himself. He sipped his drink and then hit the intercom button.

"Let's fly, captain."

We zoomed across the runway and were airborne quickly. It was my first time in a jet and was quite different than anything I'd ever experienced. We laughed and talked all the way to St. Thomas, which eliminated virtually all the nervousness I had pent up.

When we landed, there was a car waiting for us that took us directly to the shopping area. We journeyed through a number of stores and shops, buying whatever we wanted and being careful to select all matching outfits.

The car then took us to a docking area, where a huge, luxurious boat awaited. Maliek spoke to the gentleman standing beside it and nodded to me. We climbed on board and coasted away from the dock. It took us about an hour to reach a secluded island that was absolutely gorgeous. The wind was blowing through the trees, and the sand was pristine white. There were also umbrellas planted all over.

We walked to a large cabin that sat in the middle of the island. An island native came out to greet us.

"Maliek, what appenin' mon?" he said, as he took our bags for us. The two of them embraced.

"Pierre, this is Jada," said Maliek. "Jada, this is my main man Pierre."

Pierre took my hand and kissed it.

"Nice to meet you American Queen," he said.

"Watch yourself now," Maliek said, and they both started laughing.

"Everything is set up for you," he told Maliek. "If you need me, I'll be in my cabin."

There was another cabin sitting behind the one that Maliek owned. Pierre lived there during the summer months, but maintained the property year round. After Pierre left, Maliek told me to make myself at home.

I observed the cabin and it exquisitely decorated and arranged. I was seemingly in a daze as my eyes fixated on the fireplace, daydreaming about he and I sharing a passionate exchange.

"Jada," he called out to me. "What are you thinking about? Come on – let's get changed and walk to the beach."

Maliek's body was chiseled perfection. He had a beautiful six-pack stomach, a perfect chest, and manly legs. I wore a two-piece that matched his trunks, and a mini-skirt over my suit. We walked barefoot along the shore.

"Maliek this place is beautiful," I said.

"I'm glad you like it," he said. "That's what I'm here for – to make sure you are happy."

We found a spot under an umbrella not far from the water. I wanted the water to hit my feet, so Maliek spread our extra large towels underneath the umbrellas and we lay in the sand with only our heads resting on the towels.

Maliek rolled over to kiss me and I could feel his body brush against mine. Both our heartbeats increased and our breathing got heavier. Before long we had shed our matching outfits and were completely overtaken with passion. Before we knew it, we had rolled partially into the water. Afterwards, we wrapped ourselves up in towels, and Maliek picked me up and carried me inside the cabin to the bubbling, hot Jacuzzi tub.

We relaxed in the water, having been drained from a long day of traveling and activity. Once we regained some strength, we sat down to a lovely dinner that Pierre prepared for us. We fed each other from our plates and enjoyed every morsel of what we were able to eat. After dinner, we walked along the shore again holding hands and stared into one another's eyes.

Later, we resumed our passion from earlier, as we could not get enough of one another. I was in pure bliss as I drifted off with my head resting on Maliek's chest. He'd planned to show me the rest of the island, but we couldn't tear ourselves away from each other long enough to leave the cabin. Before we knew it, we found ourselves boarding the plane again.

We sat close and nestled together the entire way back to Detroit. We had gained a closeness that was beyond comprehension. With my head on his shoulder, Maliek stroked my hair and spoke.

"Baby, I have something to ask you."

I lifted up my head and looked into his eyes.

"Since Chi Chi is leaving and all, I want you to come and stay with me. Please tell me you won't have to think about it."

Before I could answer, we were locked into another passionate kiss. We continued our island experience at 33,000 feet in the air. It got a bit noisy and we alarmed the pilot a bit. Maliek assured him that everything was fine.

"So are you going to answer my question now?" he said.

There was no way I could tell Maliek anything but "yes."

"But I need someone to maintain my condo," I said.

"Don't worry," he said. "I'll have someone keep it up every week for you."

After we landed, Maliek drove to my condo, walked me to the door, and we held each other for about 10 minutes before finally letting go.

"Well baby, I have to get back to business," he said.

I stood there watching him walk back to his car, still totally captivated by him and everything that had happened. Chi Chi had entered the living room with a smirk on her face.

"Girl, look at you," she said. "You're glowing all over. And look at your tan. I know something went down this time."

"Yes, it did," I laughed. "Too many times," I said as I walked to the bathroom. "After I get out of the shower, I'm going straight to bed.

"What about your stuff?" Chi Chi said.

"Don't worry about the bags," I said. "I'll take care of them tomorrow. And we'll talk tomorrow too."

I left her standing in the living room in suspense. I was too tired to get into any details.

CHAPTER 19

My alarm clock went off and I hit the snooze button three times before dragging myself out of bed. While I was lathering up in the shower, I thought about how this would be the last week in my condo for a while, maybe even permanently.
I reminisced on the whole experience I'd just had with Maliek. Everything about him still lingered about me and wouldn't let me go. My mind was now in a seesaw back and forth, thinking back to when I'd finished college and when I'd first gotten my condo, and then forward to the present, where I now prepared to move into Maliek's beautiful mansion. I had become so content with where I was and really saw myself as doing quite well.
In fact, I was doing pretty good. I had a great job, budgeted my money well and saved and bought the condo whenever I could afford it. I also took my time to save and buy quality furniture and other nice things. I was actually quite comfortable. Now I wondered how I was going to adjust to my new home, living in that huge house, sleeping next to Maliek every night. *Snap out of it,* I told myself. It was time to get to work.
I got to work and Mr. Hall was standing in front of the bank as usual. We greeted one another and then Mr. Hall called for me to come closer so he could get a look at me now that I was back from my trip. Everyone knew about my new man. Mr. Hall looked me over a few times as if inspecting something.
"Girl, you dun went and done something," he said. "You glowin'. I'm and old man who dun been around a long time and I can tell by that look. It reminds me of the look I used to see in my wife's eyes."
"You might be right Mr. Hall," I said. I started walking towards my office.
Mr. Hall was a nice old man. He was kind of like a father in the way he talked with me. I loved my father so much growing up. I can remember all the little talks we'd have. I was his pride and joy and he did everything he could to make sure I didn't want for anything. My brother, Aaron, and I were so blessed to

have such a loving father like him. I sure did miss him. He would have been proud to see my brother go pro because he and Aaron would always play flag football together.

Around 11 o'clock, as I was sitting at my desk, I noticed a familiar scent come wavering into my office. I looked up from my desk and Rev. Turner was standing before me.

"Good morning Ms. James," he said.

"Good morning Rev. Turner," I said. "What can I do for you today?"

"I didn't mean to interrupt anything," he said. "But I'm in a big hurry and I need you to deposit this $50,000 in the account that I recently opened."

"I've got the deposit form right here," I said.

He signed and gave me a check.

"Thank you and have a nice day Ms. James," he said, as he walked out.

When I noticed that I didn't give him a receipt, it was too late. He was already getting into his car. I returned to my office and could still smell his cologne in the air. *Why does his cologne smell so good?*

I had so much work to do that I worked all the way through lunch. I really needed a nap. I don't know what Maliek did to me to have me so tired. Then I thought to myself that perhaps it was getting to be about that time of the month for me. Five o'clock couldn't come fast enough. When it finally did, I stopped by the store to buy some chocolate because I was having a chocolate moment.

When I got home, there was a box sitting on my dining room table. I called Chi Chi to find out where it came from. She told me that the delivery guy had just come shortly before I arrived home and that she'd signed for the package.

I sat everything down and opened the box. My eyes widened as I beheld a 5-carat diamond necklace to match the earrings that Maliek had given me. There was a note that said *Thanks for a wonderful weekend – you don't have to pack any of your things Saturday because I'm sending a moving crew over. Love, Maliek.*

If only I could figure out what to do with this man. Chi Chi walked back into the dining room and I knew it wouldn't be long.

"Girl, let me see that necklace. Oh, Jada! This is beautiful." She put the necklace up to her neck and looked at herself in the mirror on the wall.

"You must have really whipped it on him over the weekend to get something like this."

"Whatever," I said. "Did I show you the earrings to match this?

"No you didn't," she said. She followed me into my bedroom.

"Girl, I'm so happy for you and I want you to call me two or three times a week to keep me posted on your new love. If he starts to change, then don't tolerate it for one minute. Sometimes men start out like knight in shining armor and then all of a sudden become a stranger to you. I'm not saying Maliek will, but just in case he does, get out, because I don't want to see you hurt."

I knew she was right and gave her a big hug. I told her I loved her and how much I appreciated her advice and concern. Once Chi Chi left, I knew I wouldn't have her to come home and talk to. So far though, I was really feeling Maliek and wasn't anticipating any problems.

"I have to run to the store," Chi Chi said. "Do you need anything?"

"No, I'm good right now," I said.

After she left, I grabbed my phone and dialed Maliek. He answered on the first ring.

"How's my lovely lady doing?

"Ok - just sitting here thinking of the beautiful gift you sent me. Do you ever get enough of surprising me?"

"As a matter of fact I don't," he said. "We have only just begun, Sweetheart."

I put my hand over my heart when I heard him say that.

"Thank you Maliek. I love it. And thank you for arranging the movers to pick up my things because I was about to get busy, along with Chi Chi, to get packing."

"Well, don't worry about that. I don't want my new girl lifting a finger to do anything that she don't have to. I'm your man and that means I got this."

I was melting inside at his words.

"And Jada, it's strange that when my phone rang, I was just thinking about calling you, and that's the way I want this relationship to work. I want us to feel each other's moves and thoughts. I can't recall having such a weekend on my island like the one we had. Don't' get me wrong, I have been on several excursions, but none takes the place of the one with you."

"Maliek, that is so good to hear," I said. "I want to be the original one."

"Trust me girl - you are, Jada," he said. "I have to leave town for a few days and I'll have your keys and gate code delivered to you by Friday, but I will be back late Friday night. So, all you have to do is come home after Chi Chi leaves, and I will be waiting on you."

"Ok, I guess you have everything in order Mr. Man," I said. "Have a safe trip and call me when you get a chance."

"Ok, I will," he said. "See you soon."

After we hung up, I sat there thinking about the term "come home." This was like a dream: going to live in a huge mansion with a man who seemed to be so perfect so far.

CHAPTER 20

I could not believe how fast Saturday morning came. The movers arrived at seven o'clock sharp. They were so organized and efficient. After everything was loaded up, Chi Chi and I stood in the middle of the floor.

"I'm going to miss you so much," she said. We were both crying pretty hard.

"I'm going to miss you too," I said. We hugged as if we weren't going to ever see the place again.

I kept repeating to myself, *Jada, you are not letting your condo go.*

"Girl, you know I hate goodbyes," I said.

We cried the same way every time we departed for extended periods of time, but we always seemed to get back together. Forever friendships are like that.

"Why don't we just say 'see you later,' rather than 'goodbye?'" I said.

We walked to her truck, our eyes bloodshot red.

"Girl, you know we will always be best friends, no matter where we are," she said, hugging me again.

Just go on and get out of here before I start crying again," I said.

She started her truck and pulled off, waving her hand as she slowly disappeared. I watched my friend until she turned the corner and felt a deep sadness. We had been friends since junior high school, shared all the same classes and had met one day in the lunch room.

We started spending the night over one another's house and going to the movies to hang out. She had come over one evening crying and revealed to me that her mother and father were talking about moving to Atlanta. That was a sad day for us, but somehow we both ended up at the same college and reunited again. After college we separated again for a time but Chi Chi eventually followed me when I moved from Lansing to Detroit. Now, we were separating again.

And this time, the big change is that I'm moving in with Maliek, a major life transition. I left the movers outside of my condo and told them to go ahead with the transport. Once I got into my car, I hesitated for a few minutes before pulling off headed to my new home, *Montana Estates*. When I arrived, I sat in front of the gate before punching in my code. *Why am I making this sudden move? I guess I am lonely to the point where I want to try something different. There's one thing for sure, if things don't work out, I can always go back to my home.*

I drove through the gate and my demeanor lightened up. I saw Maliek standing in front of the house, waiting to welcome me to my new home. As soon as I got out of my car, he grabbed me and gave me a long, deep kiss, and told me to get back into my car so that he could show me my parking space in the four-car garage.

"Jada, you can park here – and the other three spaces are yours too."

After we exited the garage, we walked inside and he showed me different parts of the house, taking me to various closets and familiarizing me with everything that I'd need to know. It seemed like some of the closets were as large as the bedrooms in my condo.

The next few weeks were so lovely, as Maliek was more than a gentleman. Some weekends we held and loved on one another. The master bedroom was our sanctuary. Maliek took me on so many trips I lost count. Sometimes even one-day shopping trips to New York, Chicago, and sometimes Atlanta. Of course I'd get to see Chi Chi for a few hours whenever we were there.

One day, we were on our way home from a short trip and he asked me if I would mind taking a few trips on his behalf because he was thinking of opening up some new clubs in different cities. I never even gave it a second thought. I traveled to meet his business partners, dropping off briefcases from time to time. There were never any questions asked, as everything would always be already worked out before I got there.

I traveled for Maliek all the time and still maintained my job at the bank. He mentioned me quitting my job on several occasions, but I would stick to the same line each time he brought it up: "No Maliek - I am not quitting my job. I know you can take care of me but I just can't do it. I can't imagine not having the excitement of going to the bank every day."

I knew his money was large, and never thought about questioning him about anything. I was making him happy and he was making me happy.

CHAPTER 21

My very first birthday being Maliek's woman rolled around, and when I came home from work, Maliek had everything laid out for me. When he heard me drive up, he came out and tied a blindfold over my eyes. He walked me to the garage, took the blindfold off, and there sat a red corvette with a big bow on the top.

"Jada, now you have four stalls: you have a Benz and a Corvette. From this day forward, expect every year to add another car for your stall.

"Oh Maliek, I love you thank you."

And I really did love him. I gave him a deep, passionate kiss and hugged him.

"Maliek, I don't know what else to give you."

"Just our love is good enough for me," He said and started undressing us both. He sat me on the hood of my new car and pulled me all the way to the end to against himself. Quickly we were engaged in a passionate session right there on the car. We collapsed in pleasure after an intense exchange.

Once we our composure back and went inside the house, we danced all night to Luther Vandross and Will Downing. It was one of the best birthdays I have ever had. I loved Maliek so much that I couldn't stand it when he wasn't home or whenever he'd be away on business. I would lose my appetite until he returned. I was caught up in this man's love-web and it just kept on spinning.

CHAPTER 22

One evening I was driving home from work and realized that I hadn't been to church in a while. Every time I would talk to mom, I would say "I'm going next Sunday," and she would say, "Jada you know better; what kind of man are you so into that you can't give God any time?" When I reached the house, I couldn't wait until he came home. When he finally did, I asked him about attending church with me, and he gave me a look that I have never seen before.

"You can go but I'm not interested in going at this time. Maybe in the near future I will, but not now."

I don't know what happened but something had to have affected Maliek for him to respond the way he did. Still, I didn't pressure him. I went the following Sunday but felt so ashamed because I hadn't been in service in such a long time. I had to remember that God always welcomed us, no matter how long it took for us to return.

I went to Liberty Temple, where Rev. Turner III was pastor. When I walked through the door I could feel the love. When he asked the visitors to stand, members came from everywhere to hug the visitors and shake their hands. His message was "If Plan A Doesn't Work, God Has A Plan B." It was so fulfilling. There was a young lady that walked up to me and asked me if I wanted to attend a singles group. She gave me a card that read "Sis Gayle." When I reached my car, I saw Rev. Turner come out of the side door. He walked up to my car looking like he'd just stepped out of GQ magazine. And of course I smelled his cologne once he was close.

"Ms. James, I saw you talking to Sis. Gayle, and when I looked around you were gone." "

"Yeah I figured it would take me another hour to shake your hand so I decided to leave."

"How did you enjoy the service?"

"Rev you are so awesome."

"Well don't make this your last time coming to see us."

"Oh I won't."

He finally let my hand go and opened the car door for me. I drove away. *Why do I have this feeling like I have a connection to this man?*

When I got home, Maliek had left a note saying, "Jada I will be out of town a few days. See you when I get back. Love you, Maliek."

I was upset. I thought I was going to have a nice quiet evening at home with my man. Well I should have been used to it by now. I wondered sometimes just where this relationship was going. We'd been together for quite some time now and he hadn't asked me to marry him. I had all kinds of rings with emeralds and rubies but not an engagement ring. Maybe he was getting a little too comfortable with me.

After I'd undressed and put on something more comfortable, my telephone rang. I got real excited when I saw Chi Chi's number on the caller ID.

"What's up girl. I haven't heard from you in a couple of weeks. What's going on?"

"Yes Jada. I have some news that will blow you away."

She loved to do that to me.

"What is it Chi Chi?"

"Well you know the guy that I told you I was dating that plays pro baseball?"

"Yes, Ray."

"Well he asked me to marry him!"

"What! Girl when?"

"I was sitting at his game and my name scrolled across the billboard in front of everyone. It said 'Chianti will you marry me?' One of the commentators walked up to me with a mic and I told him 'yes.' Everyone started clapping. Girl you should have been there."

"What girl – you sure?"

"Jada, I think I'm ready for a new life. I am surprised you haven't heard about it in the media. I was crying my eyes out. My mother and father were there with everyone else, standing and clapping. They love Ray — or they could be trying to get rid of me."

We started laughing.

"Chi Chi I am so happy for you."

"I knew you would be. Thank you. Just say that you will come down and be my maid of honor."

"You already know the answer to that question."

"Good then. I need you to come down in a couple of weeks to help me shop for dresses. I'll hire a consultant to take care of the rest. And I'll book your flight for Friday after next if that's ok with your man. Oh I forgot you got your own jet to travel in."

"Well girl, I don't know what Maliek has planned that week, so book the flight anyway."

"Ok, I will call you with the flight information."

We hung the phone up. I was excited for her but feeling sorry for myself. Chi Chi had gotten a husband in such a short time and I had been living with Maliek longer than she'd known Ray. I hoped that some of all this would rub off on Maliek when we go to the wedding.

CHAPTER 23

Maliek was traveling back to Detroit from one of his business trips, having a conversation with one of his business partners.

"No man don't ever question me about my girl. No I am not going to tell her to change her appearance every time she travels; have you lost your mind? She don't question me and I am not about to bother her. Matter of fact she don't know all of my business and I don't feel good about it. I've made up my mind. No more trips for her. It's a done deal!"

He hung up the phone still heated. He thought about how wrong he was having Jada make trips for him and had never thought about the consequences. He would have a fit if anything ever happened to her. He realized that she was different from everyone he had encountered. She was just plain pure.

He really admired that she never questioned him about why he was going out of town or how long he would be gone. His exgirlfriend, Tajuana, had everything going for her, but her nagging and jealousy was unbearable. So, the day she questioned him, was the day he dismissed her, and that's why he had developed deep and meaningful feelings for Jada.

When Maliek arrived back in Detroit, he drove home from the airstrip thinking about his goddess. Once he got inside, Jada was sitting in the hot tub with her head laid back relaxing, wearing a pair of shades. Maliek undressed himself quietly and slid into the tub without her even noticing. She jumped up.

"Maliek where did you come from? She hugged him tightly and kissed him.

"Daddy is home," he said, smiling grabbing the back of her head kissing her again and again.

"I missed you," he said.

"I missed you too. It seems like your trips are so long."

Maliek stripped me of the little I had on positioned me just how he wanted me. We made passionate love.

"Jada I want you to take some time off so I can take you to Paris."

"Maliek I have never been to Paris."
"I thought I told you that this was a new beginning."
"Yes baby you did and the answer is yes."
"I am already excited (Mo Foi)."
"Really?" I hit him on the shoulder.
"Maliek, don't tell me you speak french."
"Here and there."
"You will have to teach me some french one day."
"Sure."
"Maliek, I have some news for you also. Chi Chi has gotten engaged to the guy she was dating and she wants me to fly down to go dress shopping with her. She also asked me to be her maid of honor."
"Jada, that's good news. Is she marrying the baseball player?"
"Yes she is."
"That's a short time."
When he said that, it struck a nerve.
"What do you mean it's a short time? Is there really a time limit to love?"
I pushed him back so I could get up.
"What is your time limit? Five, ten years?"
I grabbed my towel and robe and started towards the house.
"Jada wait a minute," he yelled.
I kept on walking. Once I reached the room I jumped into the shower. The water steamed my body while my tears streamed down my face like a faucet. How dare he leave me hanging about marriage? When I jumped into bed, I felt Maliek ease in behind me and wrap his arms around me.
"Jada, look at me. I didn't mean that I will never marry you or that you are not worthy of it. I just think you blew what I said way out of context. This little disagreement, we need to let it go for now. When the time is right we will talk about this."
He kissed me and told me
"I love you."
"I love you more"
"Goodnight Jada," He said with a final kiss
"Nite Maliek."
He held me all night.

CHAPTER 24

After that little disagreement, Maliek started coming home earlier from the club and spending a lot of time with me. This was the second week of him doing so and I was due to go to Atlanta Friday. He was acting like we were married and on a honeymoon. We made love all over the mansion. He must have had some kind of feeling that I wasn't coming back. He just didn't seem to realize that I wasn't going anywhere. I stopped by the club on the way to the airport. I found him on the first floor looking fine as ever, talking to Ali. As soon as he saw me, he stopped.

"Hi baby you are looking really good."

"I am on my way to the airport to go to Atlanta."

"Jada why didn't you tell me you weren't going to use my jet?"

"Maliek I didn't know what you had planned and Chi Chi made all of the arrangements; so I let her do her thing. When the idea came up, she probably didn't think about it."

"Ok, well I will let you go ahead and leave this time. But when the wedding comes, you will not be using other people's airlines."

"Ok."

I left it at that. He was very serious. He walked to the limo. We stood there kissing for a few minutes.

"Have a safe trip and hurry back."

"Are you coming back tomorrow?"

"No. I wont be back until Sunday."

He looked at me like he had to think about it.

"Ok."

He hugged me and stood there until I got into the car. He put two of his fingers to his lips and blew me a kiss as we drove off. When I reached the ticket counter, I saw a large white man staring at me. He looked real peculiar. I thought I noticed him outside when I got out of the limo. He was right behind me now and it looked as if he was getting on the same flight as me. I chalked it up to coincidence. Once we landed at Hartsfield Airport, Chi Chi and her mom were waiting. They spotted me first.

"Girl look at you," her mom said.

"You look wonderful."

Chi Chi and I screamed like kids. We hugged each other over and over, took a few pictures inside of the airport and walked to the parking lot. I loved Chi Chi's mom. Our mom's were a lot alike. They both treated us as if we were their own. We arrived at her parents' house in Marietta. They had a lovely home. We walked inside and her dad, Mr. Wilburn greeted us. He hugged me.

"Good to see you again."

"You too."

Chi Chi grabbed my hand and led me to the backyard to the side of their pool. Mrs. Wilburn had a buffet set up. The grill was still going. They had bbq ribs, chicken, potato salad, cole slaw, pasta salad, greens, cornbread and several different cakes. We were waiting for Raymond to come.

"Thank you so much Mrs. Wilburn." I kissed her on the jaw.

"Girl you know this is your home away from home."

Chi Chi's fiancé arrived. It was the first time we actually sat and talked. I gave him the third degree, asking him all sorts of questions. Chi Chi kept giving me a look like "don't do it." She should have known I would. He seemed to love her, but she seemed to be the one who was most fond. I just hoped everything worked out. We ate so much that we couldn't move, and the food was so good. After Raymond left, we talked until both of us fell asleep. It seemed as if we were having one of our sleepovers. I thought about Maliek. I missed him already.

CHAPTER 25

As soon as CJ had arrived for work the day after his date with Chi Chi, he walked through the door as usual and started his normal routine. He walked behind the bar and started looking in the coolers. Ali walked up to where he had started his count.

"Hey man, Maliek wants to see you right away."

CJ threw his hands in the air with an attitude.

"For what? I've got to get started with my inventory."

"No you don't man. Don't touch nothing. Go see the big man like you were told."

Now CJ really had a problem with the way he was approached. He started towards the elevator and Ali was right behind him. He touched the elevator and the door swung open. He stepped on with CJ looking at him very strangely. Once they made it to Maliek's office, Ali stood outside of the door. CJ gave him a very nasty look while he knocked.

"Come in." Maliek replied. "Have a seat CJ."

He sat on the burgundy leather chair directly across from Maliek. Maliek was sitting straight up with his hands clasped together.

"Yeah you wanted to see me?"

"On the real man, I want to do more than see you, but I am going to be very nice about this little situation you created. Now tell me what happened on your supposed to be date with Jada's friend Chi Chi?"

"Nothing happened, what are you talking about?"

"I'm going to ask you in another kind of way because you don't seem to know what I am talking about."

Maliek looked straight into his eyes. He was a firm believer that if you look into someone's eyes, then you can tell if they are telling the truth or not.

"Did you try to rape the young lady that you met in my club or not?"

"Man I didn't try to rape her – she was the one who tried to lead me on. You know how these women are that come in here and get their drink on."

Maliek held his hand up

"Hold on a minute. I run a decent establishment and the people that come here are decent and respected. So don't give me that crap like she was a hoe or something. That girl wasn't a hoochie. They were both decent and we know better. Those two fine young ladies were fresh out of college, just as innocent as they come. I could even tell by watching them that neither one had street knowledge like you or me. I'm really surprised at you up in here acting like you really have it together. I didn't know that you get drunk like that."

"Man is that what she told you?" CJ said. "That lying . . ."

"Save it CJ. You must have forgot that I have a monitor and was watching her and Jada; so that means I was watching you too. You was all up in her grill. The girl couldn't even breathe. I only have one solution for you. I'm not going to let no one come up in here making my club look bad or ever bring heat in here. You can check yourself into a rehab or get as far away from her as you possibly can."

"Man I don't need no rehab and I can't afford to take off work. I have bills to pay."

Maliek stood up.

"I have a club to run that I built from the ground with my money. Mine. If you go to rehab I will pay you and if and when you come back you can bartend."

"Forget it," CJ said in a smart tone.

"Ali?" Maliek called. Ali opened the door and stepped in.

"Escort this clown out of here before I get mad."

"Man you can't do this to me. You will be sorry."

"What?" Ali said grabbing him by his arm and leading him out of Maliek's office towards the elevator.

"Let my arm go," CJ screamed.

Ali grabbed it even tighter. CJ continued to talk trash but it didn't matter, Ali had him. Once they got off the elevator Maliek called Ali and told him to give CJ some money. Ali pulled out a wad of money and gave it to CJ.

"This is your last money from here." He shoved him out the door.

CJ walked to his truck heated and embarrassed. Once inside his truck, he threw the ten one hundred dollar bills on the passenger seat.

He thinks just because he has all of that money he can just get rid of me that fast. I'll show him one day who the man is. He hit himself in the chest with his fist. He drove to the nearest bar and got wasted. Afterward, he fell asleep in his truck and stayed there for hours until his neighbor knocked on the window.

"Man are you ok?"

CJ came out of his nod with blood shot eyes

"Yeah I am."

He got out of the truck, went inside, took a shower and crashed into his bed.

CHAPTER 26

When CJ woke up, it was 12 noon the next day. He had a banging headache. He took some aspirin and grabbed his throbbing head. *I've got to figure out a plan*, he thought to himself. *Maliek is not going to get away with this. Maybe I can find a way to get my family back too.* CJ lost his wife and son to his drinking and abusive behavior. *I'll just go back to my old ways like back in the day.* No one crossed Charlie Jackson, and soon, Maliek would find out who he is messing with. *I have a secret that will blow his whole world apart.*

He looked in his top drawer and found his telephone book. He went into his living room, picked up his cordless phone and quickly dialed the number of an old acquaintance he knew would do anything for a dollar.

"What's up Doug?"

"Man I haven't heard from you in ages. How are you?" Doug replied

"Yeah I'm ok but things are a little rough right now. Have a job that you might be interested in and we are talking big bucks. Can you meet me around 6pm at Captain's on the eastside?"

"Yeah I can do that."

"This is not a social call so come alone."

"Alright."

CJ walked to the corner store to get a newspaper. He loved to shop at his neighborhood store. It was a family owned business and they knew him very well. As he walked through the door, Ms. Henry was standing at the cash register reading the paper and smiled at CJ.

"What's the matter fella? You look like you are a little down today."

"No I'm just going through something right now; plus I am not feeling well today."

He walked down the aisle and picked up some soup and crackers and walked back to the counter. After ringing up his items she gave him the bag.

"I hope you feel better."

"Yes ma'am. Thank you."

He walked out the door. Once he got home, he warmed up his soup, sat at his table and went through the newspaper, searching for an area outside of town. Then he thought about another old friend of his, named Les, who used to live outside of the city. He used to take his friend drinks some days when he wanted to get drunk and get away, but Les had passed away six months ago and he had no family. At one time he was trying to get CJ to purchase his house. He said he wanted to move into a highrise, since the house required too much upkeep and that his health just wouldn't allow him to do the work.

CJ helped him with his yard on a number of occassions. CJ grabbed his Nike hat and left the house. He drove south of town, then got off on M163 and drove a quarter of a mile down, then made a left onto a dirt road. There sat the house his friend owned. He became saddened at the sight of the house, knowing that Les was gone. One thing was for sure, there wouldn't be any noisy neighbors around. CJ was his only family. He drove up the driveway and turned his truck off.

Yeah this was perfect. It was in the middle of nowhere. He got out of his truck and walked to the back of the house. He gave the back door a hard push and it opened. He went inside leading to the kitchen, stopped and looked around. The place looked the same, just a little dusty. The furniture was still covered. He walked up the steps leading to the bedrooms, and went into each of them. *Perfect.*

He walked back to his car and proceeded to Captains. He got there at a quarter til 6pm. He was early, so he sat in his truck and waited as he listened to some music. At 6pm he glanced at his watch and Doug was pulling up. He parked right next to CJ. CJ reflected on how back in the day a person could pay Doug to do just about anything. You could have him follow anyone and find out any information. Doug could also get secret information about anyone. They used to call him a Street P.I. Doug stood at the passenger side. His knock brought CJ back from his thoughts. He popped the lock and Doug jumped in.

"Whats up man?"

They gave each other the elbow and dap.

"Nothing much," CJ said. "Man I am going to make this quick. I am having a little problem with my Ex-boss."

He went on to explain the situation to Doug, telling him all about Chi Chi and how it cost him his job.

"Man my boss is loaded and I have come up with a plan that can get both of us paid, and I'm not talking about small money. We are talking millions."

"Yeah I feel ya, but tell me how do I fit into this situation?"

"Well he is with Chi Chi's friend Jada and he had her moved into his mansion; so that only means one thing: he has fallen for her. She works at a bank downtown and she travels a lot for him. I can see she is so naïve that she doesn't know what he really does for a living. She probably thinks all he does is run a club. He is making a mad killing. I want to really tell you more about my wife but this not the time. Doug, I want to kidnap his girl for some large ones. How does that sound to you?"

"You say millions huh? Are you sure he is going to pay that much for her?"

"Trust me, he will and he definitely won't go to the cops or call them. I know him. He is a very private man and if he goes to the cops, it might bring out something about him. Cops are not his motto."

Doug looked at CJ and began to count what he could do with that kind of money.

"Count me in man."

"I need you to start following her and studying her every move. You would know her at the bank. She is the only African American that works in management. She drives all types of cars: Benz, Corvette or Lexus. Plus, she's as fine as wine."

Doug looked at him with a wide smirk on his face. Doug was half white and half black and loved checkin' out sistas.

"Don't look like that man aint no funny business going on so don't even think about touching her. I don't want to hurt her; I just want to get her for some collateral."

"That sounds good to me." They shook on the deal.

"I'll call you when I get the things we need and a new cell phone for you."

"Alright CJ I'm on it."

He got out of the truck and got into his car, blew his horn and drove off. CJ sat for a minute thinking that he couldn't have found a better person for the job. He trusted Doug because they had worked together before and got away with it. He had never heard anything in the streets about it. The only problem Doug had was partying with women and maybe wouldn't be around long enough to spend the money.

CJ drove to the liquor store, got his Jack Daniels for the night and drove home. He still had some phone calls to make. He got home, went through his phone book and found his old friend Danny boy. He knew that Danny could get his hands on anything illegal no matter what it was. He dialed the number after taking a few swigs of his bottle of Jack.

"Yeah let me speak to Danny boy."

"Who dis?"

"Man this is CJ."

"Who?"

"I said CJ. What's up?"

"Ohhh, CJ what's up man? I thought you had left town or something. I haven't heard from you in I don't know when."

"I've been around. Man I need you to look out for me some heat and some of those masks you used to sell and a vests."

"Man what you doing getting ready to rob a bank or something?"

"Naw man. And another thing, I need two burnt out phones."

"Just when do you need all of this man? I don't do so much of that kind of hustling anymore. I got a new hustle. I make more money but I can get that for you and you know this is gon cost you a little bit man."

"I don't care what it costs. Just get it for me, and I will not take no for an answer."

"Ok CJ. I tell you what, meet me on the corner of Mack and Bewick tomorrow at noon."

"Alright then. Word."

They hung up. CJ stripped down to his boxers, sat on his couch and drunk himself to into a slumber. He drifted off, muttering to himself incoherently about getting his wife back and giving her some of the money he was about to make.

CHAPTER 27

CJ woke up bright and early. It seemed as if he had an instant burst of energy. He jumped in the shower, shaved and picked out a nice Enyce jean suit with snake skin boots. After getting dressed, he stood in the mirror admiring himself. He had a habit of doing that when he was in a good mood, especially if it got him money. He rubbed his hands together.

"When I get this money I'm going to buy everything I need and more."

He went into his kitchen and pulled out the breakfast items to cook.

"Just maybe I will get me a naked maid to bring me breakfast in bed."

He scrambled some eggs and fried some sausage to make a sandwich. When he was done, he grabbed his key and a Nike hat and headed out for the hardware store to purchase some things they would need. He purchased locks, string, duct tape and gloves. The clerk rang the items up.

"Will that be all sir?"

"Yeah."

He paid her and gave the clerk a nasty look. CJ had a tendency of getting paranoid. I guess it was the way the clerk looked at the items he was buying. He grabbed the bag off the counter and left. The clerk looked at the other clerk and asked "what's his problem?"

It was almost noon, so he drove to the east side to meet Danny boy. He drove around the block a couple of times, and found a parking spot. After he turned his truck off, he got out and walked to the corner where some guys were standing around. As he approached them.

"Have any of you seen Danny Boy?"

"Who did you say?" One of the guys asked.

"Who are you and where do you know Danny Boy from? You ain't the police are you?"

CJ pulled on the front of his jacket.

"Do I look like the police?"

Well a lot of people don't look like the police but they are and we don't play that around here. I'ma call him and see if he knows you and you better hope he do.

He dialed Danny Boy's number and asked him if he knew a CJ. He came back and told CJ that Danny Boy was on his way. CJ walked back to his truck. After sitting there for a few minutes, Danny Boy walked up the street. He started yelling his name. CJ beckoned for him to come to him. Danny Boy walked up and jumped into his truck.

"Man you are a little early. I have never known you to be on time for nothing."

"Cut all that out, do you have the stuff or what?"

"Man you know I don't roll like that; take me around the corner on Harding St."

CJ drove him around the corner. Danny Boy opened the door

"Wait here, I will be right back."

He came back with a backpack on his shoulder. He got into the truck.

"Here is everything you asked me for."

CJ searched through the bag to make sure everything was there and paid him. Danny Boy counted the money.

"Man you know I should charge you more than this but this is cool. If you need anything else you've got my number."

"Alright."

Danny Boy got off the truck and CJ drove off. Once he got into traffic, he got one of the phones and dialed Doug's number. Doug hesitated to answer since he didn't see a number on the caller id. He held the phone up to his ear.

"Meet me at my house."

When CJ got home, he found Doug there waiting for him. He rolled his window down after pulling in the front.

"Get in Doug."

Doug got into the truck and they drove to the spot.

"Man how did you find this place?"

"Don't ask too many questions. Trust me when CJ plans something, it's going to be handled."

They got out, went in upstairs, installed the bolt locks and got everything in order. CJ turned to him as they were walking down the stairs.

"Man I don't want no slip ups with this because we are not dealing with no fool. Maliek is a very powerful man and he knows the streets like the back of his hand. He has plenty of connections. You are to call me every move you make and don't make any hasty decisions. We will snatch her at the right time. I suggest that when you get your money, you get ghost."

"Man I don't know what I'm going to do. It's party time."

"Don't be no fool."

They drove back to his house and Doug left. CJ chilled out for the rest of the day with "Jack" since they were now best friends.

Doug went to his favorite spot. He felt like tricking tonight being all excited about the money he was going to get. Once he arrived the strip club, it was not long before he picked who he wanted and left.

After CJ drank enough, he went into the bathroom, stood in front of the mirror and noticed he was losing weight. *I've got to get myself together and start taking better care of myself. I sure do miss my wifey. If she don't want me with all of the money I will have, I can have anyone I want. No more getting fired or rejected. I'm the man and I will be my own boss from now on.*

He was startled by the phone ringing. He went into the living room and tried to figure out where the ringing was coming from. Then he remembered the burnt out. He picked it up off the couch where he had thrown it earlier with his jacket. He knew who it was. There was loud music in the background.

"Yeah Doug?"

"Oh I don't want nothing, I was just testing the phone. I'll call you in the morning when my job starts. Do I get overtime?"

"Stop playing Doug, this is a serious matter."

CJ hung up and he could tell Doug was going to be a fool with the money. Seems like he had started partying early.

Too late to cancel him right now, he thought

The next morning, Doug called CJ to check in.

"Man I am sitting in front of the bank and looks like our little prey is leaving work early"

"Man don't do nothing stupid or noticeable. "

"Ok man. You don't have to worry. I got this. They don't call me PI for nothing. I have earned that title. I was just calling you to let you know I was checking everything out."

"Ok but do not forget Maliek is no dummy. If he thought someone was watching her, you wouldn't be able to get within five feet of her."

"Yeah I hear ya."

Doug continued his watch.

CHAPTER 28

Doug called CJ.

"Man guess what, I am sitting in front of club stallion looking at your ex boss. He's hugging his girl. She is about to get into a limo. It appears she is taking a little trip. I followed her from her job a couple of days and this man is large. I didn't go all the way down but from what I can see, his place is out of sight. Nothing, but money. I am just keeping you posted."

"Cool."

Doug sat in his grey van and watched the limo pull off. He fell three cars behind them. She was heading to the airport. The limo pulled in front and Doug parked and locked his van and hurried inside the airport. There she was standing in the Delta Airlines Counter. He got right behind her and heard the agent giving her the gate number and where she was going (Hartsfield). He bought a ticket and boarded the same plane with Jada. She caught his stare and looked the other way. *Boy she sure is pretty.*

The two hour, forty five minute flight was very smooth. Once they exited the plane, he noticed a super fine sister and an attractive older woman greet her. They took pictures, while he acted as if he was reading a newspaper. He kept pace with them as they exited the airport. Once he saw them get in a sharp white caddy, he jumped into a cab and followed them to Marietta. He jotted down the address and told the cab to take him back to the airport, where he rented a car and checked into a hotel. Now that he had the address, he was straight. He went shopping to buy some things he needed, since this was a spur of the moment trip. After leaving the store he called CJ.

"Man you won't believe where I am."

"Where?"

"Atlanta. You told me to stay with her and I guess that meant I got to take a mini vacation. When we landed, there were two ladies who met her at the airport, so this wasn't a business trip." He described the two women to CJ and he automatically knew that it was Chi Chi.

"Yeah that was the one who got me fired. I should make you snatch her but never mind her for now. I'll deal with her later. I wonder what the occasion is."

"I don't know CJ. I am just doing my job. I'll call you later."

Later on, Doug drove back to the address and saw a few cars parked out front. He noticed a limo and a guy that plays pro ball, get out of the limo and go into the house. He waited outside for hours, got tired and drove back to the hotel.

CHAPTER 29

Jada and Chi Chi got up early and had a good breakfast. The two had to get an early start. They drove down to Peachtree to a professional seamstress that her consultant recommended for the bride and maid of honor dresses. It didn't take long, just materials and fittings. After they were done, they walked to The Underground discussing shoes. Chi Chi told Jada that since she had the material, she would do that another day. They did a little bit of shopping and headed back to the car. They were both worn out.

"Girl at least my flight don't leave until twelve o'clock tomorrow and that will give me a chance to get some rest. And that means no talking all night Chi Chi."

"Girl I know you are not saying that I'm the one to keep you up."

"Umm for real that would be you."

They drove back to Chi Chi's parents' house, showered and jumped into bed. The next day, Jada said her goodbyes to Chi Chi's parents and Chi Chi drove her to the airport. The wedding was only a week away. She boarded the plane and noticed the same big guy that had gotten on the plane with her the other day. She felt a little uneasy but thought maybe he was just a tourist. She dozed off and slept during a good portion of the flight. When she got off the plane, her limo was waiting but she happened to look out the window and saw the same six foot, blonde hair and blue eyed man staring at her while talking on a cell phone. It was starting to feel less and less like a coincidence.

When she got home, it was still kind of early but she got into bed and fell asleep. She didn't notice when Maliek came home but remembered him cuddling and kissing her. The next morning he slept in and she knew he was tired. Jada was looking forward to the trip to Paris after Chi Chi's wedding. She got dressed, kissed him and left for work. If it was left up to Maliek I would never work, but Jada would be bored if she didn't.

CHAPTER 30

Doug had arrived just in time to see the two women leave. Chi Chi was driving her black Expedition. He'd followed them all the way to down town ATL to Peachtree. He'd parked and watched them go into a wedding dress shop. After he saw them come out, he'd decided not to follow them while they walked in another direction. He was tired, so he decided to go back to his hotel and catch up with them the next day when the flight left at noon.

He was on time boarding the flight. He tried to turn his head, but noticed her giving him a peculiar look. He acted like he didn't see her. He sat three rows away from her. When the plane landed, he walked out of the airport behind her. He called CJ and told him she was getting in a awaiting limo.

"I made it back safe and I assume that your little friend is about to get married to a pro baseball player."

"Is that right? You mean she went all the way to ATL to give it up? She could have given it to me. Now I'm really mad and she act like I tried to rape her."

"Man I sat in front of that bridal shop forever while they played Cinderella. Now that we know she's back, we can carry out our plans."

"Well just be cool man. You are doing a good job. We have to have the right timing if you know what I mean."

"Alright CJ, I will talk to you later. I am going to get me some after watching them fine things for a couple of days."

"You are crazy. Bye man."

CHAPTER 31

The week that I was to fly to Atlanta for the wedding was a little stressful for me. I was worried about everything being set in order for Chi Chi. I sat at my desk thinking that maybe I should have just taken this whole week off. I had a responsibility to her and also to my man. He was out of town most of this week. But we did get a chance to spend some time together. When he came home, he kept saying he would make up for it when we went to Paris the following week.

It seemed as if Maliek and I were developing the bond that I had been searching for since I was able to know what love was about. I kept thinking about how tomorrow we would be flying to Atlanta to my best friend's wedding and how time really doesn't wait for anyone. I was so happy for her.

I called my hairdresser to see if she could give me a pin-up wedding style. It felt like I was the one getting married. The closer it got to Chi Chi saying her vows, the more jittery my nerves got. I tried not to keep calling her but I dialed the number anyway.

"Girl, are the dresses ready?"

"Yes they are and stop worrying so much; I have everything under control. We can pick the dresses up at four thirty tomorrow."

"I just wish that I was already there but I will call you and let you know what time we will be leaving."

"Ok Jada, I have to go I will talk to you later and thanks for being my friend."

After we hung up, I felt real special. Look at the both of us all grown up and getting married. Next, we will be having children. I really hate I wasn't able to make her bridal shower but she had a going away party she will never forget. My thoughts were interrupted when I saw Mr Leonaski coming towards me with a stack of papers. He walked in and closed the door.

"Hi Mr Leonaski."

He sat down.

"Wow, what is this all about I thought to myself."
"Ms. James, you know you have really proved to this company that you are a loyal and outstanding employee, and there is a senior position coming available. I think that you have been downstairs long enough. I would like you to consider taking that position."
"Mr. Leonaski, I don't know what to say."
"You don't have to say anything at this time; just think about it. You would love it and you would have a large office upstairs with a view of the downtown area."
"Thank you sir."
"Don't mention it."
He smiled and walked away. Mr. Leonaski had been a great boss. When I first started working with Chase, I used to wonder who the short man was, who was always wearing a navy blue blazer with grey pants. His hair was receding and brown on the sides. The only thing he had going was his green eyes. He would walk back and forth as if he were looking to see if I was doing my work correctly. I would always catch his stare. My co-workers told me he didn't mean any harm. They said that was the way he was and I would get used to it. Turns out they were right about him and I did get used to it. He only wanted to make sure that his bank was running smoothly.
My phone rang and it was Maliek. He wanted to see if I was available for lunch.
"Yes I will be taking my lunch in about twenty minutes."
"Well I'm outside waiting for you."
I grabbed my Coach bag and headed for the door. My Romeo was sitting there in a white Jag looking good as usual. He got out and greeted me with a kiss and opened the door for me. Maliek drove me to my favorite Italian restaurant. When we arrived, he must have set everything up. We ordered our food and all during the meal, seemed to have something on his mind. I cleared my throat, and looked at him with a now it's time for questioning" look.
"Maliek what's the occasion baby?"
"Do I have to have an occasion to take my favorite girl to lunch?"

"No it's just that you don't usually pick me up and take me out to lunch."

"Well baby I do have something to tell you."

I could tell in his eyes that he was about to drop the bomb on me.

"Jada, I don't think I can make it to the wedding with you. Something very important has come up and I just can't avoid it. Matter of fact, I will have to leave in a couple of hours. But my pilot will fly you to Atlanta. Now don't look like it's the end of the world. This is something I simply can't help."

I grabbed my bag and told him I was ready to go, leaving him at the register to pay for the meal. He walked out shaking his head. We got into the car.

"Maliek, the one thing that is important to me, you can't take time to support me? So I am just supposed to go all by myself while you run off to God knows where? Just take me back to work."

He drove towards the bank while I stared out the window. I could feel he was watching me. He grabbed my hand and began to rub it.

"Jada the reason I asked you to move in with me is because I know I am a very busy man so by us living together we could spend more time together. You are blowing this way out of proportion."

"Maliek, It looks like I am the business woman running and ripping for you whenever you want me to. I don't even know what my life is becoming."

I must have struck a nerve because he pulled the car over to the curb. After the car behind us passed he started kissing me.

"One day baby, neither of us will have to do any kind of work, and we can just travel the world and enjoy each other."

I melted at the sight of his sincerity. He was charming me again. After he dropped me off, I felt better and my day went by real fast.

CHAPTER 32

The next morning I woke up at six o'clock. I had so many things to do before I had to leave, and I wanted to stay on schedule. After I showered and got dressed, I could see Sung was up early cooking. I didn't have to have breakfast, but if I didn't get to my hairdresser, Deb, on time, she would have a fit.

On my way to the hair salon, Maliek called me to tell me to be on the airstrip at 2pm.

"Are you upset with me Jada?"
"No baby it's just something that just happened."
"Well Jada, you know that I love you, right?"
I hesitated before saying yes.
"Well I still will try to meet you in Atlanta."
"Ok I will call you from my hotel suite."
"Ok baby have a good flight."

I finished my appointment and arrived home just in time to get to the airstrip at ten minutes til two. I boarded and let the captain know I was ready.

"Ok Ms. James, enjoy your flight. This should be a nice day to fly."

We took off smoothly. My flight was two and a half hours and Maliek had arranged for a limo to pick me up. How could I stay mad at a man like him? Chi Chi had rented a whole floor in the Hyatt Regency for me and most of her guests. The hotel was very lovely and the suite I checked into was beautiful and had a lovely view. The Hotel also had a mini mall downstairs. She couldn't have picked a better place. I called Chi Chi to let her know I had made it.

"Well I have some bad news for you."
"I am listening."
"Maliek is not going to be able to make it but he said he would come if he could."
"Girl that is not bad news, It's ok."
"Yeah, it's your big day tomorrow and we are not going to let anything spoil it no matter what."

One thing was for sure, Maliek made sure I was accommodated. My limo driver was paid for the whole weekend. I had him on speed dial.

"As soon as I get settled I will be right over."

"No you won't; I will come to the hotel to pick you up so we can do some last minute shopping. I have called the seamstress and told her we will be there at 5:30."

"Ok cool."

Chi Chi came to the hotel to pick me up and we drove straight to Flora's Dress shop on Peachtree. The dresses were ready, and when Chi Chi tried her dress on it was beautiful. It was white satin with pearls and lace. We picked out a real tiara with diamonds. My dress was fuchsia. This lady was multitalented. She made everything you could wear in a wedding. If Maliek could see me in this dress, he would probably marry me on the spot. We both looked like the fabric was melted onto our bodies. We finished up and left to pick up our shoes. We were all set, stopped and had a light lunch, because Raymond and his teammates were giving the couple a banquet in the evening and we didn't want to be too full. Chi Chi drove me back to the hotel.

"Chi Chi, come in with me so I can give you a gift."

I had purchased two gowns from Saks Fifth Avenue before leaving Detroit. When I gave her the bag, she pulled the dress out.

"Jada you didn't have to spend this type of money for a gown."

"Yes I did."

The two gowns were so different than average gowns. They were cut with the back out with spaghetti straps. She hugged me.

"Girl you know you look out for me."

"Yeah and there is nothing too expensive for you."

We gave each other hi fives.

"We are going to give it to them tonight. Detroit style."

"Girl I have to go," she said.

I walked her to the door and hugged her again.

"See you tonight."

After Chi Chi left, I called Maliek, but he didn't answer. I guess he was busy, so I left my suite to go check out the stores downstairs. I was really impressed with what I saw. I bought a couple of silk scarves. I have a hard time passing stores without buying something, and now that I can spend my whole check on myself, it's shop, shop, shop. I went back to my room, got dressed and called my driver.

We drove to one of Buckhead's Finest Banquet halls. It was extravagantly decorated. Chi Chi and Raymond were standing at the entrance greeting everyone. They looked lovely. I admired the way the dress looked on her. I winked as I approached them.

"Hey you two look good together."

"Thank you," He said grabbing her waist.

There were a lot of couples and women were holding on to their men like you wouldn't believe. I caught many of them giving the "don't look at my man" look. Raymond introduced me to most of his teammates, and if I didn't have a man like Maliek, I would have gotten lucky this night. I smiled while he introduced me as Chi Chi's best friend and maid of honor. Chi Chi and I finally got some time to talk, while Ray walked someone outside.

"Girl I don't know why these women in here are giving me that look. I have a man and a top of the line one at that."

"Girl don't worry about them. Did you see the look on that one girl's face he introduced me and you to called Tasha?"

"I know my mind wasn't playing tricks on me."

We both laughed. The banquet turned out to be really nice. I learned in a short time that these pro ball players sure know how to party. We said our goodbyes and I headed back to my suite to rest. Tomorrow was the big day.

CHAPTER 33

The wedding was held at St. Paul Cathedral Church. It was a very large church in Buckhead. I arrived and went straight to the room reserved for the bride. There she was, standing there looking like a princess.

"Well girl, this is it. This is the happiest day of your life."

"Yeah Jada, it is now. I am all good. My makeup artist has been waiting on you."

I sat down and let her do her work on me. This chick was good. Not that I wanted to wear so much makeup, but this would be good for the pictures. I got my dress on and it was time. The wedding procession was so beautiful. It consisted of twelve groomsmen and twelve bridesmaids, myself included. Chi Chi's whole wedding party was dressed in fuchsia and hot pink and white. We stood, while the two repeated their vows. All of a sudden, I saw people turning their heads towards the door and whispering. I looked up and saw Maliek entering the church. My entire face lit up.

He was dressed in all white and was too sharp for words. I winked at Chi Chi. After their vows, Chi Chi got a long kiss from Raymond. I thought he would never let her come up for air. I wished they would hurry. I wanted to fall into Maliek's arms. Finally they finished, and when I turned to find Maliek, he was standing behind me. He grabbed my waist.

"You miss me?"

I turned my head and kissed him on his lips. He congratulated Ray and Chi Chi and passed them an envelope.

"Baby what's in the envelope?"

"Ten-thousand dollars. This is the way we do things."

I was so proud of my man. He is still full of surprises. I kissed him again.

"There is no one like you. "

After they realized what it was, they got excited and thanked us.

"It's good to have friends like you all," Raymond said.

Raymond and Maliek were not friends but I guess he felt a bond because of Chi Chi and I. They didn't stick around long. They left for their honeymoon to Acapulco. Maliek and I went to our suite and retired for the night. We had a trip of our own the very next day.

We ordered room service the next morning. We laughed and talked until we boarded *Montana 1* at noon. We were on our way to fabulous Paris.

"Baby we might as well get comfortable. We have a long flight."

We watched movies, fed each other strawberries and creatively enjoyed some whip cream. Maliek had his way with me as we escaped to Paris. Sometimes I just couldn't believe this man. His loving and attention was mind boggling.

CHAPTER 34

We finally landed in Paris. This was the most loveable place that I had ever been. It was kind of foggy because it was early morning. It didn't stop the rays of light that shone all over the city. We exited the jet and there was a Rolls Royce limo waiting to take us to the Waldorf Astoria. When I was a little girl I used to dress up in my mother's gowns and hats pretending that I was in Paris. My father would take pictures. He would put them in the family album and write "Princess Jada" under each photo. My dream was now a reality.

"Bonjour," said Maliek to the front desk clerk.

The clerk seemed pleased that Maliek spoke french. Our suite was in one of the towers and it overlooked the entire city. Maliek picked up the menu to order room service. He ordered smoked salmon and scrambled eggs. I didn't know what to order so he ordered for me.

"Maliek where did you learn to speak French?"

"Jada every brother out there is not just out of the streets. Detroit is my home but I have learned for years to venture out; and when I started finding out how people lived in other countries, I learned to appreciate what I have."

He walked over to where I was standing and hugged me.

"Jada can you get used to this?"

"Yes I can Maliek. I am loving this already. I can only get used to something like this with a guy like you."

"It better be with me," He said giving me the eye.

We went horseback riding, and even took a carriage around the city. We toured different places every day. We were greeted and treated with royalty by everyone and they really loved the fact that Maliek could communicate with them. I had never experienced another side of love before I came to Paris. Maliek had awakened something in me that I never knew. Being in Paris was so romantic. We forged a bond that will never be broken. Maliek took me shopping in various high-end stores, and we bought everything from souvenirs to jewelry.

On our last night we rode a train to Venice. We were in a private cart which was reserved for lovers only. Maliek held me closely as the train sped down the tracks. Soon our snuggling turned into unbridled passion and we were at it again, right there on the train. Of course, no one knew exactly what went on during the train ride.

The train came to a stop and we decided not to get off for a tour. Maliek composed himself and notified the conductor we would be doing a turn around. When Maliek came back to the cabin, we made love over and over again. I experienced the best love making I had ever had. As we exited the train we agreed to name this cart "Chateau Montana." It would forever carry memories.

We boarded *Montana 1* early. Once we took off, I waited until we could unfasten our seatbelts. I pulled out a box I had been waiting to give him.

"Baby I have something for you. Maliek gave me a sly grin.

"No Maliek not that. *This.*" I pointed at a box I'd pulled out.

One evening while Maliek was napping, I quietly went out to find him a gift. I really didn't know what to get him because he had so much, but I also knew that whatever I bought him would be sentimental to him.

"Here you go baby."

I passed him the box. You should have seen the look on his face. He opened the box and pulled out the emerald and diamond bracelet trimmed with gold and platinum. It had an inscription on it that read "Love you always, Jada."

"Girl how did you pull this off? I thought I was with you every minute."

He kissed me. For someone to buy *him* something was different, and he was very appreciative.

"You want me to show you how thankful I am?" He began rubbing my legs.

"No Maliek, maybe later."

I was too exhausted to do anything more.

After we landed (it was Saturday), we were so tired from all our traveling, that we slept in all day Sunday too. Sung fixed a nice dinner for us that evening. Monday, it would be time to get back to our normal schedules.

CHAPTER 35

Jada woke up early the next morning. She was excited about this being her first day back to work after a whole week. She gained a happiness she thought she would never have. She pulled the covers back and must have awakened Maliek with the movement.

"Good morning."

They both stared into each other's eyes thinking about the last week they spent together. She got out of bed and walked to the shower. Maliek joined her.

As they dried off, Maliek kissed her all the way to the closet leading her while she walked backwards.

"Stop Maliek, I have to hurry and get dressed before I wind up having to take today off." She laughed as she pulled out the Chanel dress Maliek bought her in Paris.

"You look lovely in that dress. I know what my girl likes."

"You don't look bad yourself."

He kissed her.

"Maliek are you going to have breakfast with me?"

"No you go ahead. I will grab something later."

Maliek left, and Jada had a nice breakfast before leaving for work. When she arrived, all eyes were on her. Her boss told her to meet him in the board room immediately. She headed for the board room, opened the door and everyone started clapping "surprise!" Mr. Leonaski gave her a gold plate with her name engraved on it.

"You are now the new senior bank manager. If you would follow me, I will show you to your new office."

She was overwhelmed. She followed him to the elevator, full of smiles. He pushed the button to the fifth floor. They stepped off the elevator and made a right turn. There was a nice spacious office with a reception area.

"Ms. James, this is your new secretary, Ms. Neba Lewis. "

"Nice to meet you."

They walked behind Neba as she led them to Jada's office door. Jada placed the plate on the door and stood back.

"Congratulations Ms. James," said Mr. Leonaski before leaving.

Jada opened the door and couldn't believe her eyes. There was a long L-shaped cherry oak wood desk set up with a brand new black computer. Across from the desk was a 56-inch plasma television on the wall. Underneath was a dvd player sitting on a small shelf. To the right side, was a green leather sofa with a matching chair and a cherry oak coffee table. All of Jada's hard work was paying off.

She sat behind the desk and started getting familiar with her surroundings. She spent the rest of the day arranging everything in her new office. She called Maliek to let him know about her good news, but the call went straight to voicemail. She left him a message. She figured he would get it and call her back when he got a chance.

She was so busy that she didn't even notice that it was 5:30p.m. She finished moving her last items and left for home. She was walking to her car when she noticed a van that was parked the wrong way. She could hear the other driver screaming at the man that was sitting inside.

"Hey move that thing before you get run over."

She kept walking towards her car, her mind on getting home and relaxing. When she got home, Maliek was not there yet. She waited up for him as long as she could, to tell him about her good news, but it got too late and she fell asleep.

Maliek didn't get in until much later. He hadn't checked his voicemail because he had been trying to catch up at the club. The next morning Maliek was sound asleep, so Jada didn't disturb him. She kissed him lightly on his lips. She saw him smile.

Jada left for work. She was really excited about her new position at the bank. As soon as she parked her car, Mr. Hall was walking towards the building. He turned around and told her to park in her reserved space.

"Come here Mr. Hall."

He walked to her car, popped the trunk and pulled out a gift bag.

"I got you a souvenir."

He pulled the gift out of the bag and kissed her on her forehead.

"Thank you."

She had bought him a water-filled glass ornament of the city of Paris with gold flakes swirling about.

"I wish I had a daughter like you."

"I could be your play daughter."

She put a smile on his face. He didn't know that Jada knew that eight years ago, Mr. Hall had a daughter that battled cancer and died at the age of twenty. She never mentioned it to him, but anyone could see the pain in his eyes from time to time. When Jada gave him the gift, he looked as if he wanted to cry. The two of them walked into the bank. Jada took the elevator up to her office, thinking to herself of how Mr. Hall was a good old man. *He reminds me of my father*, she thought to herself.

She got off the elevator, walked into her office and dug herself into work. There were a lot of extra responsibilities now that she was a senior banker. After a couple of hours, Neba called her and told her she had a delivery. She walked out to the reception area and there were six different expensive plants and twelve roses with a card that said "congratulations, sorry I didn't get in early. I will have to make it up to you tonight. See you when you get home. Love, Maliek."

"Ms James the plants are lovely and it makes your office look more inviting."

"Yeah my man always comes through." He must have checked his voicemail. She was smiling and admiring the way the plants brightened up the office.

Jada took lunch at her usual time. She walked across the street to the deli. On her way back, she froze in her tracks when she saw the man she had seen on the plane when she'd gone to Atlanta. He was getting into the grey van she had seen the day before. She didn't want to jump to any conclusions but hurried back to her office and closed the door behind her.

She peered out of her office window, but didn't see the man or the van. He was gone. She did not know what to do but made up her mind to let Maliek know because this could turn out to be something serious.

She couldn't concentrate on her work the rest of the day. She kept trying to figure out who this man could be and why he kept popping up. Five o'clock rolled around and she headed home, watching her review mirrors all the way home. There was no sign of the grey van or of the man. When she got home, Maliek was waiting on her. She walked into the house and hugged him. She was shaking and tense.

"Baby what's wrong? Why are you shaking?"

"Nothing I am ok."

He grabbed her hand and lead her to the pool area where he had dinner set up. There were steamed lobsters, baked potatoes, shrimp with butter sauce and broccoli and cheese sauce.

"Baby I know that your job promotion means a lot to you and it means a lot to me too. I am sorry that I didn't get your message. I promise that I will check my voicemail often."

"Maliek, that's ok. And I love the plants and the roses you sent."

By now she was so used to getting roses. If he stopped sending them, she would know something was wrong. She loved every rose and every gift he gave her, just like she loved him. While they were eating, Jada couldn't hold it any longer. She pushed her plate to the side.

"Maliek I have something to tell you."

He stopped eating.

"I am listening."

"Well I don't know where to begin, but I have been seeing this white man a lot. I think he is following me."

"What?"

"Well when I left to go visit Chi Chi, he was on the same plane, going and coming back. Now today at my job, he was sitting in a grey van. The same big white man."

"Jada you mean you've kept something this serious from me all this time? Baby, don't ever hide anything like that from me. I am going to find out who the hell this man is and why. Tomorrow when you leave for work, I will be following you."

The rest of the evening was tense. Maliek was upset and in deep thought. They showered and went to bed early. Jada was awakened several times by Maliek's tossing and turning.

CHAPTER 36

"Baby you tossed and turned all night," said Jada.

"Yeah that really got to me when you told me about the man you saw. If I thought someone was following you, it would not happen, but one thing I don't play about is my girl, family money and business."

They had a light breakfast. Jada drank her orange juice and told Maliek not to worry. He picked up her briefcase and his and stood at the door waiting for her to finish. She walked out and he followed her to the garage. Maliek trailed her all the way to work. She parked and he got out to talk to her. They looked around and there were no signs of anyone suspicious.

"See I told you this could be nothing."

Maliek was a very cautious man. He walked her to the door and told her he'd be back at five o'clock. He walked back to his car, but before pulling off, dialed Ali and told him he wanted him to come sit in front of Jada's job and watch for a grey van. He told him that he thought someone was following Jada. Maliek told Ali that he would be coming to Jada's job at five o'clock and that he was free to leave whenever he showed up.

"Alright man you know I will be there twelve o'clock on the dot, Ali said.

"I'll talk to you later. Keep me posted."

Jada sat at her desk and noticed it was only 10:30. She was worried about how concerned Maliek had become for her safety. At 11:00a.m., she took her lunch, walked out into her reception area and asked Neba if she wanted anything from the deli.

"Bring me whatever you order for yourself."

She tried to go in her purse to give Jada money.

"No girl this one is on me."

"Thank you."

Jada walked back to her office, got her purse and cell phone. She walked to the deli and ordered two Italian beef sandwiches dipped in hot juice and chips.

She paid for the sandwiches and left.

As soon as Jada stepped out of the door, there was a gun stuck in her back.

"Don't move. Keep walking."

The grey van was parked right in front.

"Get in and if you say one word, I will fill you with holes."

Jada complied in silence. The back of the van was partitioned off from the front where the driver was. Jada couldn't see where she was going or who was driving. The driver pulled over and opened the back door. He then got into the back and tied her hands and put a skull cap on her head. She couldn't see his face because he wore a mask. It happened so fast that it didn't seem like anyone noticed she had been kidnapped. The driver got back into the van and sped off. He dialed CJ's phone and CJ answered on the first ring.

"Yeah guess what? I caught little birdie and I am on my way to the spot."

"What?" CJ said.

"Are you crazy? Man in broad daylight? You know you was supposed to wait until this evening before you did anything?"

"Yeah I know but I a saw an opportunity and nobody noticed. I told you I was on my job. I will call you when I get there."

"Alright." CJ hung up.

Jada sat in the back of the van crying her eyes out. She had no idea what was going on and why she was abducted by this man. She started praying. "God don't let my life end this way. I have a lot to live for. I am so happy and Lord I know you will let Maliek find me. I just know you will hear my prayer."

CHAPTER 37

Ali got into his Escalade at 11:30a.m. and headed to Jada's job. He looked at his watch every twenty or thirty minutes since talking to Maliek. He arrived at exactly 12pm. He parked in the bank parking lot. He looked around to see if he saw anything unusual. Maliek totally trusted Ali with his life. He not only trusted him but he took good care of Ali.

When Maliek was interviewing for a bodyguard, Ali walked in, standing six feet four inches tall and weighing 280 pounds, with a clean shaven bald head. He had a look on his face that would let anyone know that he was no one to play with. He also had references from very popular people.

Ali had only returned to Detroit after being gone for ten years. Detroit was his home and he knew the streets very well. He sat in the parking lot watching everyone that came in and out of the bank. Maliek drove up around four o'clock. He had a surprise for Jada, so he showed up an hour early. Maliek parked his Jag next to Ali and got out.

"Man do everything look ok?"

"Yeah man I have been here since 11:55. And I haven't seen anything that looks suspicious. You know I'm on it. Would you like me to wait longer?"

"No man I will take it from here."

Maliek walked into the bank. Mr. Hall was standing in his usual spot. Maliek walked up to him.

"Man I am looking for Ms. Jada James."

"Oh you must be that great fella that's making her so happy and have her all full of smiles."

"Yes, I am Maliek," He said while extending his hand towards Mr. Hall.

"If you would follow me I will take you to her new office."

They walked and got into the elevator. Once inside Mr. Hall told him,

"Thank you for the souvenir that you brought me back from Paris. I have never had the opportunity to visit Paris but now I feel like I am there every day with the glass ornament that looks like the city. I love it."

"Mr. Hall I am glad that you like it."

The elevator stopped on the fifth floor and they got off. Neba was sitting at her desk.

"This young fella is looking for your boss."

She looked up from her computer. "Ms. James left to go get lunch for the both of us at eleven o'clock and I haven't seen her since. I just figured she got tied up down stairs."

"Go into her office and have a seat and I will go downstairs and see if I can locate her."

Maliek opened the door to her office. He was very impressed with the way they had her set up. He knew she deserved it. He walked around admiring how lovely it was. He walked over to the window and looked out. He could see that her car was parked in the same spot from this morning. Neba knocked lightly before entering the room. She looked at Maliek as if she could eat him up.

"Can I get you anything?"

"No thank you."

"Ok, just let me know and I will be right out here." She walked back to her desk.

A few minutes later, Mr. Hall came in. "Maliek, its strange, I can't find Jada anywhere in the building."

Maliek's countenance changed immediately.

"Man I hope nothing has happened to her."

Mr. Hall frowned. "Why would you say that?"

"Jada just decided to tell me that she thought a man was following her. She told me she saw him outside of the bank. That's why I followed her to work this morning and told her that I would come here when she gets off. But I decided to come an hour early."

"I am the head of security here and I think I should have been told. How dare someone stalk her on these premises? Let me go check again." He rushed out the door.

Maliek dialed Jada's cell number but all he got was "hello this is Jada leave a message." Beep.

"This is Maliek. I am standing in your office waiting for you." He called her ten more times and began to get really worried. He left to go downstairs. Mr. Hall was standing in the lobby talking to Mr. Leonaski. He walked to where the two men were standing.

"Have you found her?"

"No I have not," Mr. Hall told him.

"I dialed her cell number and I got nothing but her voicemail. Maliek walked out of the bank to the deli. He didn't care about the cars blowing their horns. He continued until he walked inside of the deli. He walked up to the counter and asked about her. They knew exactly who he was talking about.

"She was here at about eleven o'clock today," the clerk told him.

He walked back to the bank. When he got inside, he heard them paging her on the intercom. Still, there was no Jada. He started to feel queasy. He walked over to where Mr. Hall and Mr. Leonaski were standing. He caught the tail end of the discussion. Mr. Hall was saying he would have put a special watch on her if he had known. They searched and searched and repeatedly dialed her number but still no Jada. He called Ali to tell him what happened.

"I'm on my way back."

Mr. Leonaski walked up to Maliek.

"We have combed every inch of this building and no sign of Ms. James. All I can tell you is that you normally can't call the cops until a person has been missing for twenty-four hours. Ms. James is a federal employee and I have no other choice but to notify the FBI. He walked to his office to make a call. Maliek stood in the lobby talking to Mr. Hall. Shortly after that, Ali showed up.

"Man what is going on?"

"Jada is missing."

Mr. Leonaski came back to the lobby. "I have notified the authorities and they should be here any second."

Five minutes later two men came through the door dressed in suits. Mr. Leonaski held his hand up and beckoned them to come.

"I am agent Jones and this is my partner agent Knoles."

Mr. Leonaski shook both of their hands.

"Can anyone tell us what went on here today?"

Maliek told them about the whole conversation he had with Jada and that he came to meet her here to make sure she would get home safe. Agent Knoles cut into the conversation.

"What is your complete name and how do you spell it? Did you two have an argument or something?"

Maliek looked at him with anger.

"Jada and I don't argue," he said in a fresh tone.

"Now don't start getting all worked up. We have to ask these kind of questions. It's part of our job."

"No your job is to find her not stand here asking me all types of dumb questions."

Mr. Hall stepped in. "This man takes Ms. James all around the world and I don't think He would do anything to hurt her. Now let's get to the real business and find her."

The two agents looked at Ali and asked.

"Who are you and what relation are you to Ms. James?"

"That's not important and why are you asking me anything. Get to the important information." He turned and started talking to Maliek.

"We would have to investigate this situation and you need to cooperate, especially if this turns out to be a kidnapping."

"I'll tell you this," said Maliek. "If she is out there, we will find her and not depend on no FBI. He and Ali walked out. Agent Jones followed behind them.

"Sir I need your number."

Maliek gave it to him without looking back and kept walking to his car. Ali and Maliek drove to the club. When they got inside, Goldie and a couple of other employees were standing talking.

"I want this club closed down indefinitely," said Maliek.

One of the guys started to ask a question but Ali put his hand up.

"This is not a good time."

Maliek and Ali kept walking to the elevator, leaving the employees confused.

"I want you to make sure everyone is out of my club. All but you and me. I don't want to see or talk to anyone."

Maliek walked into his office and stood staring out of his window. He knew someone would eventually contact him with news about Jada. He couldn't believe this was happening.

CHAPTER 38

Jada continued to sob her heart out. She calculated in her mind that she'd been riding about 35 minutes. When she heard the van come to a stop, she backed herself into a corner of the van. Doug got out and opened the back door. He jumped in the back. He could see she was not going to walk out freely. He jerked her by the arm.

"Come on sweet cakes."

"I am not your sweet cakes and why are you doing this? What do you want with me?"

"If your man do the right thing, you will make it back home safe. If he don't well that's another story."

After getting her out of the van, he took her inside and upstairs in the middle room CJ picked out for her.

"You better hope that my man don't find you first."

"Oh what do we have here? A smarty pants?"

He shoved her in the chair that was next to the bed. He walked out and called CJ to find out where he was.

"I'm twenty minutes away. I had to drive down to the hood to pick up something for the missy. I will be there shortly."

Doug walked back into the room with his mask on.

"Now I can pull this off." He pulled the cap off her head. Jada's eyes were blood shot red. She thought about how she should have spoken up sooner. How dumb of her; but that was her least concern at the moment. Now all she wanted was her freedom back and for Maliek to find her. If they wanted money, it wasn't going to be a problem.

Doug heard CJ drive up so he went to meet him. As soon as he did, Jada rushed to the door to see if she could get out but it was no use. She walked to the window and tried, but it was bolted down. She heard someone talking so she sat back in the chair. The door opened and there were two men wearing masks.

"What do you all want? You will never get away with this. You don't know who my man is."

"Shut up," Doug said.

CJ had a camera phone and began snapping pictures of her. He took her purse and started rambling through it. He took her cell phone, looked at it, and showed it to Doug.

"Yeah she has a lot of messages from Romeo," Doug said, and they both laughed.

CJ pulled out a syringe and filled it with some type of drug. Jada screamed at the sight of the needle. Doug pinned her down while CJ injected her with the drug. She started drifting away. He took some more pictures of her; then they laid her on the big, old mattress and covered her. Then they left the room.

When they got downstairs, they sat at the dusty kitchen table and gave each other high fives.

"I told you this was going to be easy money. We pulled it off. You did good. Now all we have to do is get rich or die trying," CJ said.

"Man just joking. Have a sense of humor," said CJ. " One thing is for sure: we don't have to worry about the cops. Trust me, Maliek don't fool around with the police. He is going to handle this himself."

"Man she is a fine one," Doug said, smiling.

"I told you to take your eyes off her. I have no intention of hurting her. I just want the money, and keep in mind we are not dealing with no dummy. If Maliek finds out that I am behind the kidnapping, I won't have any place to hide. He is too large.

"Man let's not dwell on that, let's just get this out of the way," said Doug. He looked a little worried.

CJ picked up his cell phone and called Maliek.

"Hello, don't ask any questions, just listen. I have your pretty little thing and if you want to see her again you will do exactly as you are told with no mistakes," CJ said, disguising his voice.

"Man, don't hurt her. What do you want? Just name it. Where is she? Let me talk to her."

"No you are not calling any shots. I am about to email you some photos of her and that is the closest you are going to get to her until this deal is settled. You are to get together five million dollars cash and no cops. I mean none of your boys or nothing. I will call you again with the instructions of what to do." CJ hung up.

Maliek printed out the pictures that he were emailed and laid them across his desk. He felt almost lifeless.

"Who would do such a thing?"

He called Ali into the room.

"Look man. I have no idea who would do something like this out of all my years of business, I have never crossed the game nor have I crossed anyone. I have been good to the game and the game has been good to me. I just don't believe this."

"Have you heard from the kidnappers yet?"

"Yes they just called and sent me these photos of her. They want five million dollars which is no problem but we need to find out who is behind this."

"Where do you want me to start?" Ali said.

"Put on rewards on the streets, no matter how much it costs; hit the streets hard. I am going to be in the mansion and wait. There is nothing I can do here at the club. At least when he calls I can be in reach of the money."

"Ok man, I am out," Ali told him, touching his shoulder.

Maliek walked out of the club, got in his jag and pulled off. He had fallen in love with Jada. He hadn't grieved like this since the passing of his mom and dad.

What will I tell her mother and brother if something happens to her? I would never forgive myself if something happens to her.

He sat in his car a few minutes before going inside. He ran into Sung on his way to his room and told him what happened.

"You have to eat something to keep your strength," he told Maliek.

"No maybe later. I am going upstairs to take a shower and wait until I hear something."He walked up the stairs into the room he and Jada shared.

Ali made secured the club, then hit the streets to find Jada.

"Stan what's up? Long time no see." They gave each other dap.

"Man if you hear of anyone buying guns or anything that has to do with kidnapping call me. There's a large reward."

"Man I am on this right now. I got you."

CHAPTER 39

Doug walked into the room where Jada was being held. Jada was laying there looking very still. He shook her

"Wake up sweet cakes."

"Where am I?" Then she remembered the injection.

He tossed her a Mcdonalds bag. "Time to eat."

"I don't want it. I don't want nothing. I want to go home."

"Well if you don't want to eat, I know you have to use the bathroom, so lets go." He helped her up and led her to the bathroom. He gave her a roll of tissue and a towel.

"Don't try nothing stupid," he said.

She forced herself to use the bathroom. Then she walked over to the sink and started to run the water. She grabbed her head. *Oh my God what have they given me?* She wet the towel and washed her face. All she could see in the mirror was a blur. She tried to wash her face the second time and he knocked on the door.

"Time's up."

She opened the door. Doug grabbed her right arm and took her back to the room. She sat on the side of the bed looking at him. Her vision was still blurry.

"How long have I been here?"

"We'll just say this is another day. You better eat so that you can look pretty whenever you see your man, well, that's if you see him at all." She threw the bag at him.

"I don't want it. I want to go home."

Doug injected her again.

She called Maliek's name several times before drifting out. Doug stood there and watched her until she was silent again.

CHAPTER 40

The two FBI agents entered the bank building the next morning. There were cameras and reporters swarming the outside. Mr. Leonaski was very upset at the publicity. He had just about had enough and let the agents know it.

"Could you all get those people out there to leave? They are broadcasting all of this, and it could put her life in jeopardy. When I called you to report her missing, this was supposed to remain quiet until we could get a handle on things. Now look what you have done. It's out everywhere. What if you scare the kidnappers into doing something stupid?"

Agent Jones asked him if they could go into his office and talk privately.

"Mr. Hall, get the rest of the security team and remove those people out of my lobby and out front."

He walked toward his office with agent Jones, while agent Knoles went out front. A black Maybach pulled up in the front and parked. A young man dressed in a nice suit with matching shoes jumped out of it and walked towards the bank. When he saw all of the reporters and cameras he walked over to where Mr. Hall was standing.

"What's all this commotion about?"

"Well, looks like Ms. James has been kidnapped from the bank."

"Are you serious?" He started to walk inside, but changed his mind when a reporter asked him what he thought of the kidnapping.

"I don't know what to say. She is a very nice lady and she personally handles my accounts. I was coming to meet with her this morning. I'll be offering a reward for her safe return."

He continued on into the bank and asked to see the manager. When Mr. Leonaski came down, he handed him a large check.

"This is a reward I'm contributing towards Ms. James' rescue. He walked out of the bank, got in his car and drove away.

CHAPTER 41

Maliek sat on a couch in his bedroom. He turned on the tv and flipped to Channel 7 News. He dropped the remote. He couldn't believe they were airing the kidnapping again. He was about to turn it off, when he saw a man dressed in a blue suit offering a reward for Jada's safe return. He stared at the TV as if he had seen a ghost. He picked up the remote and turned the TV off. He shook his head in disbelief. His mind went to the pictures of Jada again. His phone rang. It was the kidnapper.

"I am sitting looking at your lovely girl, do you want her back?"

"Yes I want her back. Is she still alive? Let me talk to her."

He put the pone to Jada's ear. "Say hello to your man."

In a weak voice she said, "Hello," and he pulled the phone from her ear.

"If you want to continue to hear that voice, then I will call you tomorrow with the instructions."

"Why are we waiting until tomorrow?"

"Because I am in charge and you don't know how it feels to suffer," the kidnapper said before hanging up.

Maliek had a feeling after he hung up the phone that he knew the kidnapper, or that the kidnapper knew him.

This will be the longest night of my life being without Jada. Maliek was in so much pain. Sung came up and brought a tray of food.

"I fixed one of your favorite. How are you feeling?"

"Sung, I will be ok when Jada gets home. I am not very hungry. Just sit the tray over there and I will try to eat later."

"Ok if you need anything just call me. I will be downstairs for the rest of the night just in case you need me."

"Thank you Sung."

His mind went back to Jada. It was a long night.

CHAPTER 42

Doug and CJ were sitting in CJ's living room talking.

"Man, I have everything set up for tomorrow, and this time tomorrow we will be sitting pretty when you get your money. I suggest that you leave for Canada and get ghost. Don't come back to Detroit right away because things will no doubt be a little hot."

"Man what do you mean leave for Canada?" Doug asked looking confused.

"Well Doug, I'm buying a speed boat for us to get into after we get the money and there is no place to go but Canada, and after that, you are on your own. I know how you like to trick and party but be smart about it. Maliek and his boys will be out here doing everything they can to find out who we are."

"CJ don't worry about me, I can handle me. Let's just get the money and live large like Maliek lives."

"Whatever man."

"Let's go check on our little prey."

They left to drive to their spot. Once they got there, they found Jada still knocked out. The drugs really were doing her in.

Agents Jones and Knoles were sitting in their office discussing the kidnapping case. They still had little information and no leads on Jada.

"As far as I can see, it looks like a vengeful act. Jada James is as clean as a whistle. I can't say the same thing about her boyfriend. But he has no criminal history. He hasn't been available at all for us."

"Well I think we should put a tail on him as soon as he comes to the club or out from the club. With the type of money he has, he won't stay in long. It's definitely exploitation for ransom. I'm sure he's handling it on his own. When he makes his move, so will we."

"Tomorrow we will start," Knoles said. He will lead us to the kidnappers."

CHAPTER 43

Ali tried to take a nap but he couldn't. He got up and left the club and drove back to the same spots he had already been to see if anyone had heard anything. He had no luck. When he got to the club where Stan hung out, Stan was standing out front.
"Man I was just about to call you. I have a little information."
"What is it man and why didn't you call me?" Ali asked him.
"Ali, man, don't feel like that, I have been on my job. I told you I was just about to call you. I heard some guy named Danny Boy sells everything that a person would need for that kind of job. I'm going on Mack and Bewitt to see if I can find him."
"Yeah you do that," Ali said and gave him fifty dollars. "Just give me a call as soon as possible."
"Alright I'm getting right on it."
Ali Drove to the mansion to check on Maliek. He went inside and walked upstairs. He knocked and Maliek didn't answer. So he peeked in. It looked like Maliek was finally getting some rest.
Jada was thrown into the van. Her face was pasted against the window with her fingers covered in blood. She wrote on the back window "help me."
Maliek was following at 80 mph. The faster he drove the faster the van travelled. They came to a bridge and there was a sign that said, "Do not enter. Bridge will run out less than ten miles."
Maliek honked his horn and drove as fast as he could. The van started hitting barricades that had been placed to stop the cars from going any further. At the end of the bridge the van plunged into the deep water below sinking slowly. Maliek stopped his car and ran to the edge screaming. "JADA!"
He woke up in a cold sweat, realizing that he'd been dreaming. He got up and got undressed. He had fallen asleep in his clothes. He took a shower, jumped back into bed and tried to sleep again. The night hours were crawling by ever so slowly.

CHAPTER 44

Ali woke up early and got dressed. He didn't rest well. He kept seeing a man in a mask in his mind. He hit the streets early and checked on the club. When he exited on the eastside, he drove to Mack and Bewick. He parked, got out and walked towards a guy who was standing in front of the store.

"Hey man – you seen Stan?" he said.

"What are you deaf or something?" He grabbed the guy by the collar.

"Man I don't know no Stan."

Ali let his collar go and walked away. He looked around and didn't see Stan anywhere.

He got into his truck and drove off.

When Ali pulled into the club, he noticed a black Crown Victoria sitting across the street. He knew it was a cop car. He got out and went inside, playing it off as if he didn't see them. Once he was inside his office, he called Maliek.

"Yeah Man I think the cops are sitting outside probably the same two cops at the bank."

"They should be somewhere trying to find Jada, but don't worry about them. When you get ready to leave, go out the side entrance. Walk over the next main street where the taxis are running and catch a taxi to the mansion. Let Starsky and Hutch wait right where they are. I'm not getting ready to let them foul this up for me and put her life in danger. They did enough with the media."

"Alright man I will see you in a minute."

CHAPTER 45

Maliek jumped when his phone began to ring.

"Well, well, well, don't tell me the king is awake waiting on a call. I better get what I want today or you can forget about your little sweetie, and if you mess this up you won't have to worry about finding her. I will have her delivered to you."

"Cut the BS and tell me where to bring the money."

"At six o'clock, you are to drive to the Bell Isle River and there will be a garbage bin. Matter of fact, the third one on the left side, drop the briefcase in the bin and walk back to your car and wait for further instructions."

"Now I want my girl . . ." CJ cut him off.

"I'm the one who is calling the shots here, and remember it's my way or no way. Come alone, no Ali, nobody. If I think someone is with you or following you, the deal is off and she is gone." The phone went dead.

Maliek slammed his phone shut, showered and got dressed. He was feeling a little at ease now. He sat on the side of the bed and looked on the side Jada slept on. He noticed her journal. He picked it up and looked in the front where she kept her mom and brother's number. He decided that it was time to call her people. He dialed Mrs. Clara James. She picked up.

"Hello?"

"Yes Hello, Ms. James, this is Maliek."

"Who, Jada's Maliek?"

"Yes Ma'am."

"Oh how are you doing son?"

"Well not too good. I have some bad news for you,"

"Oh my God what's wrong? Is my daughter ok?"

"I don't know how to tell you this but Jada has been kidnapped."

"Jada what?" There was a silence on the phone then her brother Aaron picked up. Maliek explained to him what happened. I'll call you right back my mom passed out. Aaron called him back about 10 minutes later.

"Maliek, why are you just calling us?"

"Man I have been going through and I didn't want to upset your mom. You see what just happened to her when she heard the news."

"Yeah man but I am her big brother and you should always call me if something is going on with my sister."

"I am very sorry I did not call you sooner. I hope to get her back today. They asked me for five million dollars, and truthfully man, I don't care how much it costs. I love her."

"We all love JJ."

"I am going to get her back and deal with whoever did this to her. I can't figure out why someone would do this, other than for money."

"Maliek, Jada just mentioned yesterday that something wasn't right. She felt it. You know a mother can feel when something is going wrong with her children and for Jada not to return her voicemails was too much. I told my mother she was probably on some island with you."

"No not this time, I wish we were. Tonight I will be meeting with the kidnappers and all of this should be over. I will send a ride for you and your mom to come to Detroit. Do they still have the private airstrip outside of Benton Harbor?"

"Yes." Aaron said.

"Maliek be careful and keep me posted. Take my cell number Maliek."

"I will call you later."

"Ok Maliek talk to you later."

CHAPTER 46

Maliek called Ali. Ali told him he was already in the mansion. He told him to meet him in the den. When Ali arrived, Maliek was staring out the window that overlooked the pool.

"What's up Maliek how you doing Man?"

"I don't know how I am doing but I got a call from that fool and he told me to meet him at Bell Isle River at six o'clock. He told me to come alone. That let me know that this man knows me and you. Who could this be? I am not going to worry about it; I will just make the drop in the garbage bin."

"Well you know that you are not going alone. That's not going to happen. It's my job to protect you and that's exactly what I am going to do. I'll ride laying low, so when I get a chance you get Jada back, and I'll unload on whoever.

"Ok, Ali man that's cool. I am not going to argue with you. But promise me you won't make any sudden moves until Jada is safe."

"Ok you have my word."

"Wait here I will be right back."

He walked to his family room where the wall to wall aquarium was, and hit a button. The aquarium moved to one side, slowly revealing a hidden safe. Maliek opened it, He pulled a briefcase off the shelf and placed the money inside. He only loaded the briefcase with $3 million. He walked back to where Ali was.

"We'll leave in thirty minutes. That should put us there a few minutes early."

"Ok I'm ready whenever you are."

Maliek continued to glace at his watch every five to ten minutes.

"I can't take this anymore. Let's go." They walked to the garage and got into Maliek's BMW and drove off. Ali laid down in the seat when they got close.

Maliek crept along slowly and counted the garbage bins. He spotted the one he was looking for and parked. There were very few people around. There were a few speed boats and a couple of canoes in the water. He slowly got out of the car. It was 5:58. He walked up to the bin, dropped the briefcase and walked back to his car as instructed. By the time he reached the car, the kidnapper moved fast, retrieved the case and ran to a moving speed boat. After CJ jumped in, and they were a couple of seconds away, Ali was out of the car with his gun cocked. Maliek stopped him.

"Man don't shoot."

Maliek's phone rang

"Man I kept my end of the bargain now where is my girl?"

"Don't start getting all nasty with me. Walk back to the bin and there is a piece of paper taped to the bend with the location written on it."

Maliek threw his cell phone in the car and ran to get the paper. He snatched the paper and ran back to the car. Ali pulled out and turned the interior lights on so Maliek could read the address.

"Man that's right off of M163."

They hit the expressway.

"Hurry up man – hit it!"

They got there in no time. Before Ali could park, Maliek was out of the car. There was a light coming from a room upstairs. Ali ran to the back of the house where Maliek was trying to get the door open. He shot the lock off.

"Jada, Jada?" called Maliek. "Man you check downstairs, and I will go upstairs."

Maliek rushed up the steps and saw that the middle door was closed. He kicked the door open and found Jada laying there.

"Jada? Jada?"

Her body lay lifeless. He scooped her up out of the bed and hurried down the stairs with her. Once he got her to the car, he tried reviving her using CPR. Frantic, he dialed 911. Jada had no pulse.

A few minutes later, the ambulance arrived, followed by several police cars. One was driven by the two FBI agents. They'd heard it on the police scanner. The EMT's tried to get Jada out of Maliek's arms as he sat there in a daze.

"Sir can you hear me? We need for you to move back so we can check the victim."

Ali grabbed Maliek's arms and pulled him away from Jada. They put her body on a stretcher and started working on her. Maliek trailed the ambulance to the hospital.

Ali stayed behind for a moment and talked to the agents, then left for the hospital himself. In all of the years he worked with Maliek, he had never see him cry.

Agent Jones and Knoles were the first to get in front of the news cameras, talking as if they were the ones who found Jada. *The victim, Jada James, was employed by Chase Bank before she was abducted from her job a few days ago. We have located her and as you can see, this has been a short investigation. Right now we have no word on the criminals or her condition. She has been taken to the Henry Ford medical center. Stay tuned for an update at eleven o'clock.*

The EMT's were on the radio with the emergency room doctors.

"Wait a minute doc, I have a pulse but it's very faint," said the EMT. He kept working on her. "I'm getting a heartbeat!"

They all arrived at the hospital and Maliek rushed to Jada's side.

"Baby hang on, I'm right here."

When they reached the door to the restricted area, the doctors told Maliek that he couldn't come any further, and to stay in the waiting room. Maliek walked back outside of the hospital and dialed Aaron's number.

"I'm at the hospital and Jada is in the emergency room with the doctors. She is alive and that's all I can tell you right now. It's up to God now. I'm calling you to make arrangements for you and mom. Be in Berrien Springs in an hour and I will have my pilot pick you up."

As soon as he hung up, Ali was walking up to the hospital door.

"they got her back breathing."

"Oh thank God."

They walked into the family waiting room. Maliek started pacing back and forth.

"Man calm down, everything is going to be ok. Can I get you some coffee or something?"

"No, but what you can get is the person that did this to my baby."

"Yeah you got that. I am about to start doing that right now. Just keep me posted on her condition. I'm out."

Maliek was sitting with his head in his hands when Ms. James and Aaron arrived.

"Maliek, where is my baby?"

"She is still in with the doctors. They are running her through a series of tests."

The doctor came in and shook hands with Maliek and Aaron and nodded his head towards Mrs. James.

"I am doctor Miyata. I have her stabilized. But she is still in a coma due to the drugs that were administered to her. She is very dehydrated and running a temperature, which is my main concern. We are running different meds thru her IV that will help her, but all I can say right now is that she is stable. We have moved her to the fifth floor to the ICU unit."

"Can we see her?" Mrs. James asked.

"Yes, as long as you make the visits short. She will need plenty of rest. It takes a while to recover after your body overdoses from any type of drug."

"Overdose? What do you mean? She never used drugs."

"Mama what he is saying is, whoever had Jada, gave her drugs."

"Thank you doctor," said Maliek.

"You are welcome. I'm just doing my job. Now let me show you which elevator to take."

Mrs. James went in first and Jada was laying there hooked up to a few machines with an IV drip. She walked over to the bed and kissed her on the forehead.

"Jada, mama is here. Can you hear me honey? I know that the Lord is going to bring you back. Don't you dare try to leave here without me spanking your little butt for being grown." She placed her hand over her head and said a prayer. "You are going to be alright. Mama loves you more than anything in the world." She kissed her again and walked back to the waiting room.

Maliek walked in and kissed her on the lips. She looked so innocent and pure.

"Jada can you hear me? I have never in my life had anyone like you and I never wanted this to happen to you. I loved you at first, but now I know I am in love with you. I must admit, in the beginning, I took advantage of you, having you travel with my dirty money, and never should have involved you in any of my business. I was wrong. I never even discussed any of my dirty business with you and you never even questioned me about anything that wasn't right, and I will never keep you in the dark about anything. Things are going to change for the first time in my entire life. I realize that I can love someone, and that someone is you. Meeting you has changed my whole outlook on life. I will change for you. I didn't know how much I really loved you until someone took you away from me. I will forever protect you for the rest of my life Jada; you hear me? I love you." He kissed her again and walked out.

Aaron went next. He could hardly stand the sight of seeing his sister in this condition but was thankful she was alive. He stared at her.

"JJ you have to wake up. Remember when I used to tease you and hide your little dolls? I'm sorry and I'm sorry for scaring you with the Ronald Regan mask all the time. Wake up Sis., we are all waiting on you. I don't know what I will do without you. I love you."

He pulled the blanket up around her shoulders, kissed her on the forehead and walked out.

CHAPTER 47

CJ and Doug sped across the Detroit River until they reached Canada.
"Well it's over for this boat Doug, you can have it. Do whatever you want with it. I have other plans."
"Thank you buddy." They both laughed loudly.
CJ headed toward the main street and Doug followed him.
"Wait up, you act like you are running from the police."
"I am, come on."
Once they reached the main street, they caught a cab to the most extravagant hotel in the area. The cab driver recommended the Ambassador Hotel.
They paid the driver and then walked inside. CJ asked Doug to check them into rooms with one of his ID's. He asked the clerk for an adjoining suite.
"Well sir you are lucky we have only one left. Are you a tourist?"
"Yes."
They got into the elevator and headed to their rooms.
"Man it's time to live like a king," CJ said.
"Yeah I know what you mean," Doug said grinning.
The elevator swung open. Doug gave CJ his key, which was for room 803, while his was 805. CJ stopped in front of his room and Doug stood behind him. He stuck the key in, stopped and turned around looking at Doug.
"Man can't you give a man a chance to check into his room in peace? Who do you think I am? You think I'm going to run off with the money? Give me a break."
He opened his door and Doug was right behind him.
"No man, I don't think you will run off, I just think we should get this settled right away; why waste any of our time?"
"Well if you insist; but don't stand over me man. Have a seat."
It didn't really matter what CJ said, Doug wanted his money. He was never the type to wait around after a job. He was good

at whatever the job was, but when it was time to pay, it was time to pay.

CJ sat across from Doug in the sitting area and began to count the money. He picked up the suitcase to see if he had overlooked some money.

"My eyes must be playing tricks on me."

He started counting the money a second time.

"Man what's wrong?"

"You don't want to know. That slickster had the nerve to short me. There is only three million in here."

"Count it again," Doug said.

"Man just sit down and shut up."

He counted it again, and it was only 3 million. He counted out one million and put it in a bag with a draw string.

"Well this is it."

Doug took the money and put it in his backpack.

"Well nice doing business with you." They shook hands.

"I'm going to my room to take a shower; see you around."

Doug didn't even look towards room 805. He walked to the elevator going downstairs straight out the door. An hour later, CJ sat in his room plotting his next move. He left his room and took the elevator downstairs to the front desk and told the clerk that he lost the key to 805. She didn't argue with him but gave him another key. She knew the two men were together and never questioned anything.

As soon as CJ got back on the eighth floor, he stuck the key into Doug's door and pulled out his nine MM. He walked in softly trying not to make any sounds. He walked to the bedroom then to the kitchen area.

He walked into the bathroom but there was no Doug. *Hmm. Doug is smarter than I thought.* He shook his head and walked back to his room.

Doug got out of the cab in front of the docks where they left the speed boat. He got on the boat and went back across the Detroit River. *I know he didn't think I was going to hang around with him. It's time to party.*

Doug made it back to Detroit and caught a cab to his apartment. Going into the building, he knocked on his neighbor's door. John was a college student. When Doug was away, he would get his mail and watch out for his apartment.

"Hi Mr. Brenner."

"Hey Kid, do I have any mail?"

John left the door to get the pieces of mail.

"Thank you and I have a gift for you." He passed him the keys to his Nissan Sentra.

"Thank you Mr. Brenner! I don't know what to say."

"Well don't mention it. I figure it would be easier to give you the car, now that I won't have to give you a ride all the time; and you deserve the car, pal. See ya later."

Doug went to his apartment, and before he could get settled, he heard John outside enjoying his new ride and blasting the music. He looked through his blinds and smiled. He then called him a cab to take him to CS Auto Trader. A short time later, Doug drove off the lot in a brand new red Dodge Ram truck. The one he had always wanted. He thought about buying a condo but was undecided on whether he wanted to continue to live in Detroit. He decided he would check into a suite in the meantime.

All he had on his mind was women and partying. He drove to the liquor store and bought all kinds of wines and liquor from there. He went shopping and bought new gear and a Rolex watch. He drove to the Anthem Hotel downtown and paid for a suite for one week. Doug showered shaved and got dressed in a nice pair of dress slacks with a matching dress shirt. He went to the Rolex Adult Club. Little did he know he would be making the biggest mistakes of his life.

He parked in front as if his truck were a limo. He went inside and sat in the VIP section. He starting spending a lot of money and drew a lot of attention. Doug was looking to attract a woman name Cocoa. She was beautiful and curvacious.

"What you doing when you get off?" Doug asked.

"It all depends on what you want me to be doing sweetheart."

Cocoa was a young lady that knew her stuff. She could smell money and she was a master of getting into a man's pockets, fast. Most of the guys had become her regulars. She worked for other clubs in Detroit but she had the Rolex on lock. The men loved her. After giving Doug the show of a lifetime, he asked her if she could come back to his room.

"Yes that will work," he said. She waved at the girls that stood watching wanting a piece of action.

They drove to the hotel. Once inside Cocoa turned the music on and danced all over Doug. The more she danced the more money he pulled out. Doug paid Cocoa top dollar for her company. Her G string was full of money as well as the floor surrounding her.

"Hun, did you hit the lottery or something?"

"No I didn't. Let's just say hit a little lick."

"Well I must be the lucky girl for tonight."

"Come here," he said, giving her a hug. "Yes you are."

Cocoa gave Doug a little of everything he wanted. She made about $1500 total for the night. She put the money away and got dressed.

"Would you like to come back later tonight and bring one of your friends? I need one that I can get freaky with."

"Yes Doug I know just the one to bring."

"Ok then that's another date for tonight."

"Doug its 2am right now so that's tonight."

"Ok honey looking at how beautiful you are made me forget the time."

He kissed her on her cheek and she walked downstairs and caught a cab. Doug laid in the bed thinking about the night he'd had, and drifted off to sleep.

CHAPTER 48

Doug woke up at eleven o'clock holding his head, hungover from the night before. He forced himself out of bed and into the shower. After getting dressed, he went to have lunch and drove to his apartment. When he drove up, John was coming out of the building. He waited until Doug got out of the truck.

"I love this new truck you are driving."

"Why thank you John. How's it going with the car that I gave you? Is the starter still slipping?"

"Yeah a little but it drives me to where I need to go. I can't thank you enough."

Doug walked towards the building and John pulled off. Doug went inside his apartment feeling out of place. It was nothing like the hotel. He pulled out his lockbox and put some of the money in his pocket. He decided to chill out at home and get some more rest. He turned the television on and heard a special broadcast offering a reward for him and CJ. He got a little nervous. They told the public they were looking for a black and white male. *I wonder if she can identify me.*

He got up and put his shoes on and grabbed the lockbox. He went to John's door to see if he'd made it back. He knocked on John's door.

"Hey John, keep an eye on my apartment. I will be gone for a few days; and here keep this for me. I don't trust leaving this in the apartment while being gone for a long time."

He passed the lockbox. After John took it, Doug reached in his pocket and got one hundred dollars.

"Here – for all your trouble. Maybe you can buy a starter for your car."

"Thank you. You're really looking good nowadays. Have you hit the lottery or something?"

"No I just feel like you could use the help plus you have been such a good neighbor." Doug left and got into his truck driving towards the hotel admiring the jewelry he bought for himself. He pulled into the parking lot and looked around to see if someone was following him. He went inside to freshen up. He ran water in the Jacuzzi so he could be ready for the girls when they came. Cocoa phoned her dancing buddy partner in crime, Tracey.

"Girl, do you want to get paid tonight?"

"What's up Cocoa?"

Tracey knew if Cocoa was calling, it had to be some good money involved.

"Girl I met this trick last night and he is loaded with money. With your brother not working and everything, I know you are going to jump on this opportunity."

"What do I have to do?" Tracey asked

"Girl you are not new to this game. You give the trick what he wants and he pays you. Do you want in or what?"

"Yeah, you know I want to go."

"Ok then I will pick you up shortly."

Cocoa picked Tracey up and they drove to the hotel. Cocoa told her how easy it was for her to make plenty of money. Tracey laughed.

"As in roll my body?" She rolled her body in the car seat.

"Girl come on, you know I had to put you down. You are the best candidate for the real action."

They walked inside to use the phone. Doug told them to come on up. When he opened the door, he couldn't keep his eyes off Tracey.

"Drink what you want and get comfortable."

They poured themselves some drinks. Doug had already started drinking before they arrived. He was feeling real good and was more than ready for the night to begin. He told them to dance on each side of the hot tub while he massaged his private parts. He kept his eyes on Tracey. She could run circles around Cocoa. Tracey climbed into the tub with Doug and started rubbing his back.

"What's up baby? Where did you get all this money from? You robbed someone or something?"

"Just say I hit a big lick," he said admiring her whole body.

By the end of the night both girls had made over fifteen hundred dollars each. Everyone got what they wanted. They left about 4 in the morning. Cocoa pulled up in front of Tracey's house.

"Girl thanks. That was some easy money."

"You know you are my girl, take care and tell your brother hello."

Tracey got out and waved goodbye to Cocoa. She went inside and woke her brother up who was laying on the couch.

"Wake your lazy butt up."

"Girl leave me alone." Stan had too many drinks the night before.

She threw the money on the coffee table.

"Look at all the money I made last night."

He opened his eyes.

"Tracey girl who you dun robbed?"

"Nobody, Cocoa turned me on to this trick that got a hold of a lot of money. He is just throwing it away like running water.

Stan sat up on the couch. This might just be what he had been waiting to hear. Ali was looking for anyone that might be spending a lot of money. Stan quizzed his sister on everything that happened and wanted to know all about the guy.

"He said he hit a lick."

"What? Can you get back with him tonight? If you can it might be worth a lot of money."

"I will call after twelve o'clock but for now I am tired. I will talk to you later after I get up."

Stan sat up thinking for a while. Could this be the same man Ali is looking for?

CHAPTER 49

Stan woke up early, took his shower and waited for twelve o'clock to roll around. It seemed like it wasn't coming fast enough. He started to call Ali but he wanted to make sure Tracey could contact the man first. He waited until ten minutes after twelve then he knocked on Tracey's door.

"Sis get up its after twelve o'clock. Get up and call that man, and if it's what I think, then we will hit the jack pot. Do you hear me Tracey?"

"Alright Stan, I am getting up now."

She put on her robe and walked out of her room. Stan was still standing outside.

"Dang Stan can I get some more sleep?"

"Yeah after you take care of this business ok?"

When she reached the bathroom door he was still there.

"Can I wash my face and brush my teeth?"

They both started laughing. They were really close. They only had each other. And when Stan lost his job, Tracey took up his slack. He loved his little sis. Tracey came out and dialed Doug's hotel room. She could hear some women's voices in the background.

"What's up with you today?"

"Who is this? Don't tell me my sweet Tracey called me back?"

"Yes."

"Well I tell you what, you just get your butt back over here so I can give you some more of my money."

"Honey how long are you going to be on the phone?" a voice said in the background.

"Tracey just come on over."

"You sure?"

"Yes I am sure. See you when you get here."

"It's on, and it sounds like he has already picked up some girls but it don't matter. Tracey is going to get her some more money no matter what."

"Let me see that phone, Sis."

Stan dialed Ali's phone number. He was on his way to the club.

"Man this is Stan. I may just have the man you have been looking for. My sister met this trick and he is spending mad money hanging out at the Anthem Hotel. She is supposed to see him in a couple of hours."

"What makes you think this is the one?"

"Man she said he is partying hard and say he hit a lick. He didn't say what kind but I am willing to bet on it."

"Ok, I will check this out and this better not be a wild goose chase. But call me when she get ready to leave and give me the information."

"Oh and Ali before you hang up, if this is your man, do I still get the reward?"

"For sure word is bond."

After hanging up with Stan, Ali continued to drive to the club. Just as he was approaching the street, he saw the Crown Victoria that was parked by the club. *I guess they think we are searching for the kidnappers. Why would they follow us? They should be able to catch them on their own.* He drove in front of the club and got out. He called Maliek to see if Jada was ok but didn't share the new information. He wanted to check it out first. Goldie came in right after Ali.

"Man come sit at the bar. I want to run something down to you."

He told Goldie everything that Stan had told him.

"Well you know I am riding with you man. I want a piece of this busta too." Ali fixed both of them drinks.

Tracey got dressed. She stood in their kitchen drinking orange juice. Stan was sitting at the table eating a ham and cheese sandwich.

"Tracey, my partner, Ali ,will come to the room and knock on the door and you make sure you are the one to answer it and go straight out of the door as they walk in."

"Ok I got it."

"Do not stick around, Tracey; this man has did a bad thing to my partner's boss."

"Alright, alright."

"Tracey, call me when you get out of the room and come straight home."

"Ok, ok Dad."

"Tracey I'm not playing with you. This is serious."

She smiled while getting into her Honda accord. Stan closed the door. He was on pins and needles waiting for his sister to call. He always wanted the best for his little Sis., after their mom passed, he did his best to try to help raise her. Maybe she could take some of the reward money and go back to school. She had stood by him through his bad luck spell. Tracey called him when she got to the hotel. She caught the elevator to Doug's room and phoned him outside of the room.

"Open the door I am outside."

There was another lady that opened the door. Tracey walked in to see one white girl, one asian and another black chick that kept swinging her hair. Doug really had gotten busy picking up women at every strip club. This time he had bought drugs, coke and x-pills. Everyone was as high as they could get. Doug was sitting naked in the hot tub.

"Come on over here and join the party," he said showing all his teeth. Tracey was definitely turned off.

"I will join you in a minute. Let me have a few drinks to warm up a little."

She was doing a good job at stalling the party crew. She really didn't want to undress because anything could happen any minute. She really started playing it off dancing in her clothes. She knew this really turned him on. He had plenty of women this night but he stared at Tracey. She saw three one hundred dollar bills on the floor. She danced over and picked them up quickly before anyone noticed. She stuffed them in her bag. Now all she had to do was play the waiting game.

CHAPTER 50

Stan Called Ali and told him that Tracey was inside. He wrote down the information and hung up. Goldie could tell from the look and conversation that it was the call Ali had been waiting for. The two men walked out of the club and got into Maliek's blue Benz. Ali didn't even think about the feds parked up the street. He was so excited about the lead. They headed to the Anthem Hotel. Agent Knoles and Jones saw them leave and pulled out a few cars behind them. When Ali reached the hotel, he parked in the back entrance. They walked around the front and took the elevator to the second floor, walking slowly down the hall. They could smell smoke and hear music and laughter. He looked at Goldie who had already pulled his Glock. Ali knocked on the door.

"Did any of you girls order room service?" said Doug.

"I'll get the door," Tracey said.

Tracey walked to the door and opened it. Ali winked at her. The other girls started screaming

"Shut up and get out if you want to see some more tricks," Ali said. "Raise up out the tub man!"

"Man who the hell are you?"

Wham! Ali busted him across the head, and blood started trickling down his face. Goldie grabbed him by the neck and dragged him out of the Jacuzzi.

"Now I am going to ask you one time only. Where did you get all of this money?"

Doug didn't answer. Boom! Ali hit him again, and then Goldie gave him a blow.

"I'm going to ask you one more time."

Doug threw his hand up covering his face.

"Man don't hit me again. It was CJ man. It was CJ." Ali looked at Goldie.

"Charley Jackson? Where is he?" Ali screamed.

"I don't know. I left him in Canada."

Agent Jones and Knoles ran to the second floor. Two young ladies was getting dressed as they ran up the hall flashing their badges.

"They are going to kill him," they said hysterically. They gave them the room number. The door flew open.

"Everybody put your hands in the air."

Ali and Goldie raised their hands. Agent Knoles collected the guns while Jones held his gun on all three men.

"Somebody tell us what's going on." They called an ambulance for Doug. Agent Jones took a good look at Doug's face and head.

"Don't tell me this is one of the kidnappers?"

Ali nodded his head.

"I knew that you would lead us to the kidnappers. All in just a matter of time."

Agent Knoles walked around the room and saw all the money laying around.

"How dumb. There is always a dummy in the bunch. You could have gotten away, but you are going away for a long time."

The ambulance arrived and patched Doug up. They still took him to the hospital to see if he had any permanent head injuries. Agent Jones and Knoles took a statement from Ali and Goldie and told them they were free to leave. They would get all the credit for finding one of the kidnappers. They let the team seal off the room while they followed Doug to the hospital. As soon as Doug finished testing and getting treatement, he was given medication and transferred to a federal facility where he gave his statement. CJ was put on the America's Most Wanted list. Ali called Maliek.

"Man, you won't believe who was behind Jada's kidnapping. CJ!"

Maliek was completely shocked. He was glad to find out who was behind all of this but his mind was preoccupied with Jada's condition.

"Man I will call you later. Thanks."

"Don't mention it. I will not stop until I get my hands on CJ."

Ali and Goldie drove to CJ's last known address. They walked to the back and kicked the door in. After thoroughly ransacking the house, Ali came out of CJ's bedroom.

"Look what I have." He held CJ's personal phone book in his hand.

"Let's finish and get out of here. You know the Fed's will be here soon," Goldie told him.

"Yeah they have the snitch. A snitch is a snitch. He's probably telling them this address right now. Let's go."

CHAPTER 51

After sitting in the family waiting room for several hours, Maliek stood up and asked if anyone wanted anything. No one wanted anything.

"Well I have a better Idea, I will call my driver to come and take you all to the mansion to get settled in and mom you can get some rest. Afterwards Aaron can drive one of my cars to bring you back anytime you are ready."

"Man that is a good idea. My mother knows she could use a little rest. This will take a toll on her if she doesn't."

Ms. James looked at the two of them.

"Alright. I will do it but don't think I will stay long. I will be back soon."

"Thank you Mrs. James. I will be right here by Jada's side. And I will call you right away if there is any change."

Maliek called his driver. A short while later, he walked them downstairs to the main entrance of the hospital, rolling Mrs. James' luggage behind him.

"Make my home your home."

"Son you don't have to go out of your way."

"Yes I do. There is nothing I wouldn't do to make you feel comfortable."

The limo took Aaron and Mrs. James to the mansion where they were able to finally get a little rest and enjoy some pampering. Seeing how well Jada had been living temporarily took their minds off her condition.

CHAPTER 52

Maliek walked back into the gift shop approaching the older candy striper.

"Ma'am is there any way I can buy all the balloons hanging, some teddy bears and a couple of cards?"

"You must have someone special."

"Yes I do ma'am. Someone very special to me."

She rang all the items up and he paid her.

"Would you have someone deliver them to Jada James' room please?"

"Yes I sure will."

Despite his lifestyle, Maliek knew he should be serving God. His father was a minister, and he and his brother were both raised in church. When they got older, they got in the game together. Something happened that made them drift apart. He often thought of how his parents were probably looking down from heaven and they were very disappointed that he and his brother had not spoken to each other in ten years.

He walked into the room to find the balloons had been delivered. They made the room brighter. He walked over and kissed Jada on the lips. He looked up to see her doctor come into the room. He checked her pulse.

"Well I have some good news for you and some bad news. Which one would you like to hear first."

"I want to hear it all," Maliek said.

"Well Ms. James is going to recover. I can't say exactly when but she will recover. The second thing is that she is eleven weeks pregnant."Maliek's eyes widened. "I am going to run some tests to see if the baby was affected by the drugs. So far, we have flushed most of it out. In the next few days, I will be able to tell you more. She could wake up at any time. Just hope and pray for the best. She is young and strong.

After the doctor left, Maliek pulled a chair next to Jada's bed and grabbed her hand.

"Baby did you hear what the doctor said? We are going to have a baby. She was still unconscious but Maliek was the happiest man in the hospital. "Baby can you hear me? If you can hear me, squeeze my hand."

A tear rolled down her face and her eyes began to open. Maliek smiled. "Hold on baby let me get the nurse."

Soon the doctor and nurse were in the room.

"Hi, I am Dr. Miyata. I have been assigned to you. Can you hear me?"

"Yes," she said in a weak voice.

"Are you in pain?"

She shook her head "no." He examined her again, then had the nurses unhook all the machines.

"You are not out of the woods yet but I am going to need you to take it easy and not get overexerted. You need plenty of rest and if you are feeling ok tomorrow, I will have you moved to a private room on the recovery floor. I will be back to check on you later."

"Maliek you are here."

"Yes baby I am here and I'm not going anywhere."

She dozed off. Maliek left the room to call Aaron and Mrs. James. They were very happy and told him that they were on their way. When they arrived they finally talked Maliek into going home for a while to get some rest. He called his driver to come pick him up. When he got into the car, he had the driver take him to the club first. When he got to the club, everyone could tell that things must have improved.

"Open this place up full force. Call everyone and tell them we are back to normal operation. Tell them to get to work as soon as they can."

Ali, call 92.3 FM and tell them to announce that Club Stallion is open again with no cover charge.

"Got ya. I take it that the little lady is ok?"

"Yes she is. Man she had me scared for a minute. But she is alright."

Maliek got back into his car and called Ali on his cell.

"Man, get on a hunt and find that clown, CJ. I don't care how much money it will cost or who he is with. I want him before the police get him and the people that gave you the info on his partner. Call them up and give them twenty five thousand. Tell them good looking out."

"Alright man, I am on it," Ali said.

Ali dialed Stan's number. He could hear Tracey react in the background when Stan repeated how much money they were about to get. He told them to come by the club the next day to get their money.

Aaron and Mrs. James reached the hospital. They walked into Jada's room. She heard her mother's voice and she woke up. She was sluggish.

"How are you feeling?"

"Ok." She looked at Aaron

"Boy what are you looking at?"

Aaron knew Jada was back. The nurse walked in and told them she was very weak and that they could take turns to being in her room.

Maliek got home, showered and changed his clothes. He finally ate something, which Sung was glad to see. He then rushed out the door again to get back to the hospital.

CHAPTER 53

The very next day, Jada was moved to a private room and had a room full of cards, plants, and other get-well gifts.

Meanwhile, Stan and Tracey drove to Club Stallion to receive their reward.

"I don't know how long we are going to be here," Stan told her.

"I thought we were just coming to pick up the money and leave."

"Girl just park in the lot."

They went inside and asked for Ali. Ali stepped off the elevator. He was blown away by Tracey.

"What's up man?"

"Man Ali, you remember my sister Tracey?"

"Hey Ali." She was smiling, and her eyes were glued to him.

"Come with me," Ali said.

He took them to the third floor where his office was.

"Have a seat. My man Maliek isn't here, but he really appreciates what you all did for him. This is compliments from him." He pulled out the envelope with the money inside.

"Give it to her. She is my banker."

"Here banker, you can be my banker anytime."

After Stan left, Ali and Tracey spent a good bit of the evening together at the club. He dropped her off later and she kissed him goodnight before walking to her front door.

CHAPTER 54

The day came that Jada was ready to go home from the hospital. Aaron and her mother were there waiting for her release, while Maliek went home to have a room decorated with balloons and welcome home banners. Aaron came in with the wheelchair while the doctor was giving Jada instructions on where to get her follow-up treatment.

Aaron helped her inside the car.

"Take me to my condo," Jada said.

"Stop playing Jada," said Aaron.

"Aaron I am not playing. Take me home and don't ask anymore questions."

"Aaron she is serious, just do like she said," Mrs. James told him.

"I have some things I need to work through," said Jada.

"Why every time a woman get pregnant by a man, she get an attitude with the man?" he said driving off.

"Aaron leave your sister alone. She knows what she wants and we are not going to interfere with her decision." He didn't say another word but drove them to the condo.

The condo had been kept up nicely. Her mom pulled back the covers and tucked her in. Aaron and Mrs. James sat in the living room talking.

"What's wrong with her Ma? She finally gets a good man and look how she's acting."

"Well, you don't know what's really going on between them. We don't live here, remember?"

He kissed his mom and left for the mansion. He also planned to tell Maliek the bad news.

"What's up man? I see you all made it just in time. Let me go and get my girl out of the car." He started towards the door

"Wait man. Hold up. Jada is not in the car."

"What do you mean she's not in the car? What, they didn't release her or something?"

Aaron explained everything that had happened when they left the hospital. Angry and confused, Maliek drove to the club and locked himself in his office.

Over the next couple of days Maliek, sent Sung over to the condo to fix meals for Jada and her mother. He even made sure she had everything she needed but he didn't call or go to see her. Aaron spent most of his days with them, but at night, he would go partying at the club. Jada started getting around real good. She felt better every day. She even started to dress up the way she used to, just in case Maliek came over, but he never came by. She felt sorry for playing him like she did. She missed him. She tried calling him but he wouldn't answer her phone calls. Jada had made a mess.

CHAPTER 55

Maliek sat at his desk thinking about how meeting Jada had changed him so much. And as bad as he wanted to see her, he didn't allow himself to break. He knew he'd done a lot of things, but what would prevent her from coming home? He drove to the mansion, packed some luggage and drove to the airstrip. He didn't know exactly where he wanted to go but after boarding *Montana 1,* he told the pilot to take him to his favorite spot.

"I'll contact you when I'm ready to come back to Detroit," Maliek said.

Maliek took a boat to his island. Just seeing the blue water, gave him a sense of peace. He walked towards his cabin and Pierre ran out to meet him.

"Mon what are you doing here?"

"The last time I checked I own this place."

"Oh I don't mean it that way. I just meant if you had called me, I would have fixed everything up for you. Where is the missy?"

"I have no idea. I will tell you later but I need you to go into town and bring me the usual food and plenty of bottled water."

Maliek changed into some shorts and headed for the beach. He lay in the sand under an umbrella thinking about the last time he was here with Jada. This was going to be the perfect spot to ease his mind. He stayed on the beach most of the day. He tried to keep his mind off Jada.

Pierre made it back, he grilled steaks and had dinner with Maliek. They talked about everything and Pierre's humor helped lighten Maliek's mood.

"Would you like to go into St. Thomas with me? I know plenty of island women that would love to meet you."

"No thank you, Pierre. I am not in a party mood; plus I am not ready to meet other women. I am missing Jada. She is all I want."

CHAPTER 56

The next day when Aaron arrive at the condo, Jada and Mrs. James were sitting in the living room talking.
"How are my favorite two women doing?" he said.
"We're fine, Aaron," they said. "Have you seen Maliek?"
"No Jada," he said. "I haven't seen Maliek in a couple of days."
"Well, he hasn't been home or at the club," said Jada. She stood up. "Mama, get your purse. Let's go. Aaron, take me to the mansion so I can get one of my cars and go find Maliek."
"Have you tried calling him?" she asked.
"Yes and he didn't answer my call," she said. "And I know that he knows it's me. I hope nothing happened to him."
"Jada don't think like that," said Aaron. "I'm sure Maliek is fine. Remember, you are the one who left him hanging."
"Aaron, don't start in on your sister," said Mrs. James. She winked at Aaron. He smiled as they got in the car.
Jada couldn't take it anymore. She wanted to see her man. They reached the mansion and went inside.
"Mama you might as well get comfortable because we ain't going anywhere."
She went to find Sung. "Have you seen Maliek, Sung?"
"I have no idea where he is. This is kind of strange because he always tells me if he is not going to be here. I fixed dinner a couple of days and he never showed up. But I know everything is ok."
She went all through the mansion and couldn't find any clues that might let her know Maliek's whereabouts. She then jumped in her white Lexus and drove to the club. She didn't stop downstairs but walked straight to the elevator going upstairs to his office. When she got there, the office door was locked. She turned around to find Ali standing right behind her and quickly broke down and fell into his arms.
"What's wrong, Jada? Come into my office." He guided her to his office. "Now tell me what wrong with you?"
"I can't find Maliek," she said.

"Wait a minute," Ali said. "Stop crying so that I can understand what you are saying. Did you say you couldn't find Maliek? Sit down and and let me see if I can call him."

Ali dialed Maliek's number but didn't get an answer.

"Matter of fact, Jada, I haven't seen Maliek in a couple of days. I thought you all were at home, seeing as how you just got out of the hospital." He dialed the number several more times but kept getting Maliek's voicemail. He left a message for him on the last try.

"Maliek, this is Ali, man. Call me. It's very important. If nothing else, call me and let me know you're ok."

"Jada, I don't know what to tell you," he said. He gave her some more tissue to wipe her face. "I'm sure he's alright. Just calm down and don't make yourself sick."

"Ali, he's not ok," Jada said. "I know he's not. He's not at home and I need him!"

"Well, Jada, do you really love Maliek?" Ali said.

"Yes I do," she said.

"Then why didn't you go home from the hospital?" he said.

"I thought we needed some time to think," she said.

"Uh huh," said Ali. "Jada, you shoulda saw him when you got kidnapped. I thought he was gonna lose his mind. And when we found you . . . well, I have never seen my boss shed tears."

Jada stopped crying. "He cried?" she said.

"Yes girl," said Ali. "He cried to the point where he had me shedding a few tears."

"Oh Ali, I can't live without him!" Jada said. "I love him."

"Jada, all I can tell you is that if you can't live without him, then keep looking for him until you find him." He could be anywhere. We're used to him leaving like this, but after he met you, all of that changed. I knew a time when he would leave for months."

"Ali, don't say months! Jada interrupted. "I can't do this." Suddenly Jada had a wild thought come to her head. She grabbed her purse. "Ali, thanks. I think I know where to find him." She kissed him on his cheek. "See you later." Ali sat in bewilderment, not understanding what came over Jada so suddenly.

After Jada got in her car, she called Maliek's pilot.

"This is Jada. Are you in the Detroit area?" she said.

"Yes I am Ms. James."

"Ok, meet me at the airstrip in 30 minutes," she said. "I have an emergency trip."

"Alright, see you then," he said.

He had no problem taking Jada wherever she needed to go. Maliek had given him permission to do so and told him to treat Jada as if it were himself.

Jada called her brother: "Aaron, I'm leaving town. Tell Ma I will see her when I get back."

"Where are you going Jada?" he said.

"I'm going to get my man," she said.

She drove to the airstrip and the piliot was waiting for her. Maliek didn't leave instructions for him not to tell anyone his whereabouts.

"Where would you like to go Ms. James?" said the pilot.

"Take me to where you dropped Mr. Montana off," she said.

"Ok, as soon as you get situated and fastened in, we can take off," he said.

"I'm ready," said Jada.

She was more than ready to find Maliek and could hardly wait for the plane to get to where he was and land. The flight was nice and smooth. This time it seemed like it was taking forever. When they landed, she told the pilot to stay in town for a couple of days and that she would pay all his expenses. This was good news to him.

"Thank you Ms. James," he said. "I'll be ready whenever you all are."

Jada went shopping to find sexiest swimwear she could find. She wasn't showing as of yet, and whatever she found, she was going to rock it. She knew Maliek would love it. She went to the docking area where Maliek took her before she didn't see anyone that looked familiar. But she knew she could pay someone to take her to the island. Suddenly, a man walked up behind her as she searched about the various yachts and boats.

"Queen Jada," said a voice.

It was Pierre.

"Oh, I'm so glad to see you," she said.

"How are you?" he said. "Nice to see you again."

"I need to get to the island," said Jada.

The timing couldn't be more perfect. Pierre was just coming from shopping for some seafood for Maliek. He untied his boat and Jada stood there like she was lost in her thoughts.

"Come on. You going or what?" said Pierre.

She snapped out of her daze and hurried aboard. They headed for the island.

"Pierre, can you keep my coming a secret?" she said. "I want to surprise him."

"Yes, I can," he said. "And I know he will be glad to see you. He wasn't expecting anyone and has seemed rather sad this trip."

They docked and she told him to go ahead of her. Jada watched from behind a tree until she saw Maliek leave the cabin. He walked to the far end of the beach. The sun was going down and the sky was a beautiful pink and blue haze. She slipped inside the cabin, put on her new swimsuit, and pulled her hair back into a ponytail.

Maliek drew a large heart in the sand with Jada's name in the middle. He was about to get into the water when he glanced towards the cabin and noticed the silhouette of a beautiful woman walking towards him. All he could see was a white sheer top that reached her knees and the faint outline of a two-piece swimsuit underneath. As she drew closer, he realized it was Jada.

He jumped to his feet and they ran towards one another. He scooped her up and spun her around. He then carried her to the place where he'd laid his large towel underneath an umbrella. They kissed one another with great urgency, like they'd never known of such passion.

"I miss you," said Jada, her eyes full of tears.

"I miss you too," said Maliek.

Soon they were all over one another, the passion fully ablaze after having been apart. Maliek admired every part of her, totally captivated by her beauty and perfection. Before long they found themselves rolling back and forth in the sand in the heat of passionate exchanges.

"Oh Maliek, tell me that you'll never leave me again," said Jada.

He whispered in her ear. "I'll never leave you. I love you so much. Will you marry me?"

At the height of another climactic exchange, Jada screamed out, "Yes! Yes I will marry you!"

Maliek stroked her hair as they both lay together in the afterglow. He pushed the few strands of hair that were covering her face.

"My beautiful wife to be."

They eventually made their way into the water to wash the sand and sweat from their bodies. Their session had been so intense that Jada's was still trembling, and Maliek felt weak all over. She rested in his arms for what seemed like hours.

"Baby, now tell me why you didn't come home when you were released from the hospital," said Maliek.

"Maliek, I have loved you from the very beginning and I guess I loved you more than you loved me. You didn't think enough of me to tell me about your business. It does matter now. I knew something, and that was, that you were not born rich. But by you not telling me, I felt betrayed. Yeah, I carried your dirty money, but I loved you so much that I don't think it would have really mattered if I had known. I felt like every woman should stand by her man, regardless of what he does. That's if she truly loves him. When I was in that coma, I heard every word you spoke to me, but couldn't say a word. But as soon as I heard the doctor say that I was going to have a child, something inside of me woke up and I could hear the excitement in your voice. I knew I had to fight to wake up to the life with you and the baby. When I couldn't find you, I don't want to even think about that feeling. You can never hide from me."

She kissed him tenderly.

"I don't want to hide from you, ever," said Maliek. "It's been hard for me living in that mansion without you. I had to get away. Don't ever punish me like that again."

Maliek gazed at Jada for a response.

"Ok baby," she said. "I won't."

They rolled up the towel and headed back towards the cabin. Upon arriving, they showered and sat down to enjoy the food Pierre had prepared and ready for them on the table. It had gotten cold so Maliek warmed their plates. They finished eating, got right into bed and fell asleep facing each other, their lips lightly grazing.

CHAPTER 57

The next morning, the couple woke up early to head back to Detroit. They told Pierre about their engagement and that he was invited. They would send for him and his girlfriend for the wedding.
"That's a bet, mon," said Pierre. "Congratulations."
He took them back to town, where they could board *Montana 1*. Maliek called his pilot.
"Are you sure you want to leave today? said the pilot. "Could you give me an hour?" Maliek could hear someone in the background. "Baby are you coming back to bed."
"Ok," Maliek said. He laughed as he put the phone down.
"What's so funny, Maliek?" Jada said.
"He's getting his groove on," he said. "He wants us to wait for an hour."
Jada laughed. "I guess he met him an island girl."
"That's ok," Maliek said. "We can go find a jeweler."
They then went out and found the perfect jewelry store. There was a set of rings sitting in the window seemingly waiting on them. The jeweler told them that they would be perfect for a his and her engagement set.
"Thank you Maliek!" said Jada. He bought the set and they both slipped on the rings right there in the store. Maliek had his personal jeweler at home and he had large plans for his bride to be.
They boarded his jet, and on the flight home, made all kinds of plans. Maliek decided that he had enough money, plus the money from the club, so that he wouldn't have to do anymore dirt. Once he got married, he knew everything was going to change, and that he wanted to be the model father.
When they arrived at the mansion, Aaron and mom were sitting on the terrace eating and enjoying the lovely view. They walked over from the terrace.

"Looks like we are just in time. Oh, look-a-here. I knew it! I knew it!" said Mrs. James, as she hugged them both. "Don't tell me you all eloped."

"No mama," said Jada. "We are just engaged."

Aaron shook Maliek's hand. "I knew she would find you. She almost lost her mind. Congratulations, man."

"Thank you," said Maliek.

"You know what Jada?" said Aaron. " Mama was just saying you were going to show up here engaged."

"How did she know?" said Jada.

"You know we have never been able to fool that lady," he said.

"Those rings must have cost and arm and a leg," Mrs. James said. "I'm liking that platinum and gold with diamonds. Your dad would have loved this, Jada. "Maliek, welcome to the family."

"Yeah, welcome to the family," said Aaron. "And now that this is all over, I have to hit the club. I have a hot date." He kissed his mom on the cheek. Don't' stay up too late."

"We'll see you tomorrow," they all told him, laughing.

Mrs. James knew that Aaron was always going out. He was all dressed up. She knew that his having dinner with her had only been a way to kill a little time.

EPILOGUE

The Sunday after Jada was settled back in the mansion, she and her mom woke up early to attend church. Before getting into the shower, she woke Maliek up.

"Would you like to go to church with me?"

"No Jada. I won't make it this time. Don't rush it. I know that if I'm gonna start changing, it will start with going to church. Just bear with me, Honey."

"Ok Maliek. You can come when you're ready. See you later," she said after she finished dressing. She leaned over and gave him a kiss.

When they arrived, the church was packed. However, they were able to find three seats. Rev. Turner noticed them after they were seated and asked Jada to stand.

"This is the young lady we posted the reward for and prayed so hard for the safe return of," he said.

Everyone gave a standing ovation, crying and clapping.

"You see, this is the result of how God answers prayers," said Rev. Turner amidst the applause.

After everyone had sat back down in their seats, he went on to tell a story of how his father was a minister and how he and his brother went into the street life when they got old enough. However, after having had enough of that life, Rev. Turner said that he changed, distanced himself from his brother, and eventually started preaching the Word of God.

"That's when my blessings began to flow," he said. "Now I have eternal life."

After sharing that experience, he went into his sermon, but stopped in the middle of it. He started walking down the aisle.

"You know," he said. "Ms. James is not the only one that has been blessed today. I am truly blessed also. I mean, ten long years I have asked God to reunite me with the closest family I have left."

Rev. Turner began wiping tears from his eyes with his folded handkerchief.

"Ladies and gentlemen of the congregation, I want to introduce my long lost brother," he said. "I haven't seen him in ten years."

His brother stood up in the back of the church and started walking towards him. They met in the center.

"Welcome home Maliek."

The two brothers embraced and the congregation cried and clapped loudly. Jada, Mrs. James, and Aaron each absorbed the power of that incredible moment. Jada's joy was mixed with utter shock. *Now* she knew who Rev. Turner reminded her of.

Made in the USA
San Bernardino, CA
18 June 2016